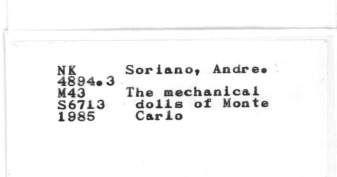

THE MECHANICAL
DOLLS
OF MONTE CARLO

André Soriano

THE MECHANICAL
DOLLS
OF MONTE CARLO

Texts by
Antoine Battaïni
and
Annette Bordeau

RIZZOLI
NEW YORK

Translated from the French by John Ottaway
Designed by Pippo Lionni
Photographs by André Soriano

First published in the United States of America in 1985 by
RIZZOLI INTERNATIONAL PUBLICATIONS, INC.
597 Fifth Avenue, New York, NY 10017

ISBN 0-8478-0679-0

Printed and bound in Italy

Library of Congress Cataloging-in-Publication Data

Soriano André.
    Mechanical dolls of Monte Carlo.

    Translation of: Automates de Monte-Carlo.
    1. Galéa, Madeleine de, 1874-1956–Art collections.
2. Mechanical dolls–Private collections–Monaco–Monte-
Carlo. I. Title.
NK4894.3.M43S6713 1985 688.7'221'094407404949 85-18336
ISBN 0-8478-0679-0

A Short History of Mechanical Dolls

Since the dawn of the machine arts in antiquity, mechanical dolls have never ceased to fascinate man. Today robots controlled by computers have inherited the place of traditional models. Japanese researchers have recently perfected a robot pianist animated by three fifth-generation computers that may be considered the modern version of Jaquet-Droz's harpsichord-playing android, so much admired in 1789. The proper word for mechanical doll, "automaton," is derived from the Greek *automatos*, meaning "self-propelled." But the word has come to mean a "machine that imitates the movement of a living creature," or, more precisely, a "device driven by an internal mechanism, which imitates the movements of a living creature."

Formal historical and archaeological evidence proves that animated statues were already known in ancient Egypt. They often seem to have been made for political and religious purposes. The Egyptians believed that the statue of a god or a dead person possessed the powers of whomever it represented, as soon as the priests had breathed a ka, or divine soul, into it, using magical motions and formulas. They alone possessed the secret of the statue's ka. In fact, it is thought that these statues were driven by a rather simple mechanism. To animate a statue in a certain way from a distance, the high priest stirred up the sacred fire. By so doing, he raised the temperature of the air in an invisible pipe that led to the statue. The expanded air pressed upon a hidden device that triggered the desired movement.

At Nepata, in south Egypt, the new pharaoh was designated by an articulated statue of the god Amon, which indicated with its finger the male heir who seemed most worth of the throne – in reality, the one most certain to be submissive to the priests. According to Herodotus, on the feast of Osiris mobile articulated statues were presented before the temples. Callixenus, a Greek orator of the third century B.C., tells us of the wonders accomplished in Egypt by a statue of Nysa, driven around in a chariot pulled by sixty men. When the procession came to a halt, the statue stood up, filled a cup with milk, and sat down again. The Louvre contains one example of these animated Egyptian statues: a mask of Anubis, a god with a jackal's head and the body of a man. The lower jaw of the mask is mobile; during religious ceremonies, the god seemed to speak to his followers, announcing oracles and predictions.

Mechanical dolls were also used for religious purposes in ancient Greece, at Delphi in particular. But at the end of the pre-Christian era, real geniuses of mechanics appeared. They invented and constructed mechanical dolls animated by both pneumatic and hydraulic means. No longer limited to religious uses, these dolls were secular and scientifically orientated.

About 250 B.C., the Greek Ctesibius, credited with the invention of the clepsydra, was building organs and other hydraulic musical instruments. During the second and third centuries B.C., Heron of Alexandria and Phylon of Byzantium each wrote several treatises devoted to mechanical dolls. Heron of Alexandria also seems to have been the first collector of mechanical dolls. He invented automatic doors for a temple and built several animated figures that have remained famous: a Hercules in combat, blacksmiths who beat their anvils in time, and even a theater with a number of self-propelled automatons. In a real sense, Heron and Phylon are the forerunners of modern mechanical dollmakers. They particularly inspired the construction of animated figures and scenes powered by water, which would decorate princely grottoes and gardens throughout the Middle Ages, Renaissance, and Baroque periods.

During the Middle Ages, the Arabs were the first to apply the principles of construction of mechanical dolls as set out by Heron and Phylon. In 807 Harun ar-Rashid offered Charlemagne a clock that was a masterpiece of workmanship and technical prowess. When it struck noon twelve windows opened and a horseman emerged from each. The gardens of the caliphs of Baghdad and of the Almohads of Spain were inhabited by mechanical dolls animated by hydraulic energy. Artificial birds capable of cheeping while beating their wings and figures who appeared to walk around aroused the astonishment and admiration of visitors. The fashion spread to Sicily, where Arabic influence was considerable in the Middle Ages. In fact, Arab craftsmen in the twelfth century built the mechanical dolls destined to animate the gardens of the king of Sicily at Palermo.

It was doubtless a visit in these gardens that inspired Robert II of Artois to design the park of his château at Hesdin in the same way. At the château, the preferred residence of the dukes of Burgundy, guests could see artificial horsemen, musicians, and of course mechanical birds. Few could restrain their admiration and stupefaction, especially after crossing a gallery that contained the jokes so amazing to contemporaries: figures that spouted water and randomly sprinkled people, five devices that sprinkled ladies who walked over them, five mirrors that produced various illusions, and a device that slapped those beneath it.

Montaigne at the end of the sixteenth century saw a marvelous grotto at Pratolino, near Florence, where "not only music and harmony are produced by the movement of water, but also several statues and doors set in motion by water do various things, several animals dive to drink, and similar things. In a single movement, as the whole grotto fills with water, the seats squirt water on the buttocks." In another Tuscan villa, at Castello, he saw "another fine grotto where every kind of animal is represented true to nature, with water fountains spouting from beak, wings, claws, ears, or nose." In the Villa d'Este at Tivoli, Montaigne was especially impressed with the hydraulically produced organ music and bird song. The music was silenced and new spectacles signaled by the appearance of an owl, also driven by water under pressure.

In France, the fashion for mechanical dolls that performed in rock grottoes came to a height at the château of Saint-Germain-en-Laye, during the time of Henry IV. The château is built on a hilltop descending towards the Seine in six successive terraces, each terrace opening onto artificial caves filled with scenes of Perseus and Andromeda, Neptune and the dragon, Orpheus, and other fantastic sights. These grottoes filled with mechanical dolls were animated by hydraulic force alone, the water descending from terrace to terrace as at Tivoli.

According to a contemporary description of the grotto of Orpheus, "You can see beasts, birds, and trees come up to Orpheus. Upon touching the strings of his lyre and hearing the harmony of the divine bard, the beasts lie down on their heads and sides, the birds flap their wings, and the trees move. On one side is Bacchus, sitting on a barrel with a cup in his hand; on the other are wonderful goddesses in the form of half columns and several other marvelous girls, whose secrets I'll keep, for others will come for the pleasure of seeing them." As at Hesdin, Pratolino, and Castello, pipes carefully hidden beneath the paving stones released jets of water that gushed unexpectedly and indiscreetly, "to fill," as Montaigne put it on another occasion, "ladies' petticoats and thighs with that freshness."

continued on page 40

7

Shepherdess with Sheep

This shepherdess, fashioned by Decamps in Paris, 1880, wears her original costume. A silk brocade skirt decorated with garlands covers a pleated petticoat of olive green satin. Her jacket of burgundy silk, with tails and pagoda sleeves, laces up the front and is set off by fine white braid and a magnificent flowered straw hat. Biscuit ware is used for the bust as well as the head of this delightful figure (1). With her deep brown glass eyes on the spectator, she offers a wicker basket, lifts the lid with her finely modeled biscuit-ware hands, and reveals a recumbent lamb, which turns its head and lets out a sonorous bleat. This animal, whose voice is astonishing, conceals beneath its leather skin a sheepskin bellows. A cam works the wiring system, which opens the bellows and, at the right moment, frees a bell-crank lever, allowing a spring to close the bellows with a single stroke. The bellows blows through a little reed like those used for toy flutes, giving the lamb a loud bleat.

2

3

4

Child with Spinning Top

The child with a spinning top belongs to a category of small mechanical dolls whose activities derive from daily pursuits. Although dressed in a sailor's suit with a small lace pocket set off by a bow tie, he wears sabots. His hair is real, made up of little tufts sewn into a crown on the top of his head. He hits his top with a whip, which maintains its rotation and allows it to move, according to the laws of inertia and precession that govern the gyroscope. The mechanism (6), placed in the base, has an original arrangement that steadies the lateral movement and rotation of the top. It is turned by a flexible cord welded to one of the axes of the fast-winding pinions. The top is fixed to the end of a lever driven by a cord on a central pulley, brought back by a spring.

5

6

This arrangement protects the mechanism
from any accident that might arise as the result of a
blow to the top. In this eventuality, the cord slips on the
pulley and the mechanism awaits the next cycle.

Countryman and His Pig

The countryman turns, raises and lowers his head, and tantalizes his pig with a superb truffle, which he moves toward its snout and draws back immediately. The pig becomes agitated, moves its head, and sticks out a fine bright pink tongue. A number of variants on this personage were made; this example is by Triboulet, in Paris, 1885. In some examples the pig is offered a slice of bread and jam rather than a truffle. But whatever the arrangement, the animal's reaction is the same: it sticks out its tongue. The mechanism is concealed in the bottom of the chair; it drives a musical cylinder and comb at the same time.

10

Japanese Bust

Nearly life size (65 cm. high), this Japanese bust rests on a base characteristic of the period of Napoleon III, reminding us of the influence of oriental art at that time. She smells a rose held in her right hand, blinks, and masks the lower part of her face with a fan, showing off all the more clearly her slightly slanted, expressive eyes. This mechanical doll is a model of flexibility with her ample, richly decorated silk clothes and above all her very fine skin. The body surfaces of most mechanical dolls are composed of papier-mâché, but this Japanese lady is covered with supple, closely-fitting leather. So smooth are her movements and her skin that one would think her a real human being, were it not for the mechanism that appears as if sprouting from her shoulders (12) when she is undressed for restoration (9).

11

12

13

14

Putting her Foot in It

This little girl with lively eyes and real hair smears her face with the piece of fruit in her left hand and puts her foot into a plate of fish. She was created by Decamps in 1890. The metal collar pierced with holes around her neck forms part of the mechanism that makes her shrug. To the collar are sewn her clothes, the compensating springs that articulate her arms (16), and the multiple axes of the pivots. The latter give considerable mobility to her arms, as her hand positions demonstrate (14, 17). Her movements are transmitted by wires inside her legs attached to a plate in her back.

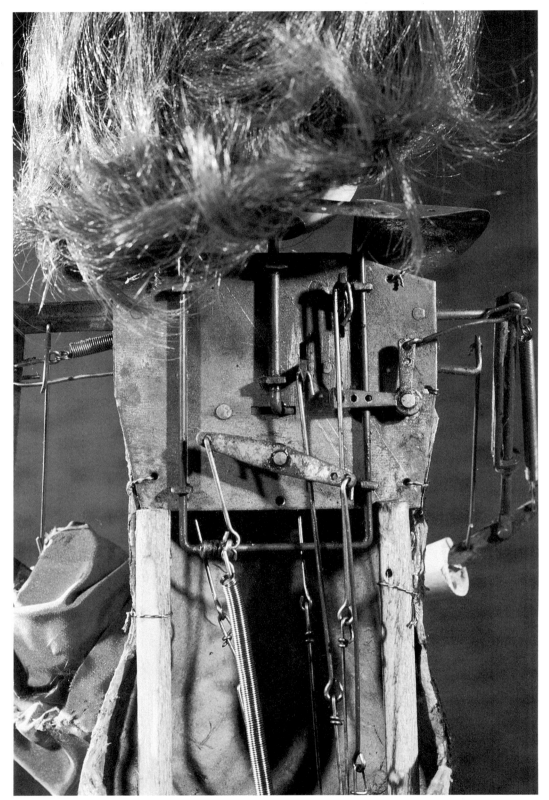

16

Snake Charmer

Zulma the snake charmer was the most successful doll
of her time: the only known mechanical doll that can
perform in the nude. Several examples have survived;
this one is by Decamps, 1890. Dressed in the oriental
style fashionable in the period, she also wears rich
jewelry and bracelets. The ornaments are of a special
utility because they hide the articulations of her arms.
Without this contrivance, it would have been impossible
to leave her arms bare. She nods her head and blows
into a horn to charm her snake, which is drawn toward
and away from her face in realistic, sinuous
movements. Her particularly beautiful face and mobile
eyelids give intense life to her expression. Her chest

CHARMEUSE DE SERPENT
DECAMPS PARIS 1900

dilates and expands in time with her breathing. Face, body, and hands are papier-mâché mixed with gutta-percha and ivorine, giving a beautiful satin finish to her skin. The standard spring-driven mechanism is lodged in a base with cut-off corners, covered with a heavily embroidered carpet. Considering the quality of the body's workmanship, it is difficult to believe that there are wires inside her, from head to the ends of arms, transmitting movements. Dressed or adorned with only her jewelry, she charms her snake to the sound of four different tunes, produced by a musical cylinder and comb.

22

23

Young Lady Powdering

This blue-eyed brunette turns her biscuit-ware head to the right and left while powdering herself with a powder puff of swan feathers, held in her right hand. Then she bends her head slightly forward to inspect the result in an oval mirror with a gilt rim, which she holds by its ivory handle. Under a violet and pink ensemble set off with lace, she wears finely embroidered petticoats. Her shoes are made of glove leather with the stitches showing. The base, in the form of a die, was frequently used by Lambert as support for his mechanical dolls; he made this one in 1890.

Young Lady with Fruit

This young lady with a biscuit-ware head, large blue eyes, and an open mouth revealing two rows of teeth, was made by Lambert in 1880. She holds a magic wand in her mobile right hand and leans slightly forward to present an apple enclosing a tiny girl in a lacy red dress, who turns around by means of the mechanism visible between the hand of the large doll and the bottom of the apple. Her olive green and straw yellow dress hides embroidered petticoats but reveals dark green cotton socks, stuck to the legs of the doll when it was made. The main mechanism is in an unusual position, concealed in the body of the doll rather than in the base.

24

25

Young Girl with Bird

This animated doll, whose mechanism is in the base, was built by Lambert in 1890. She inclines her head, lowers her eyes toward a wicker basket, and lifts its cover to reveal a tame bird that flutters its wings to a crystalline air. The bird is faithfully reproduced, with real feathers; it seems quite at ease in its satin-covered nest. The round-cheeked child is given a youthful look by the biscuit ware used for her head and hands, while the rest of her body is of papier-mâché, a technique frequently used in dolls of the period. Her open mouth reveals a row of fine teeth and her eyelids are mobile. Her long blond ringlets spread over the back of an apricot silk robe covered with black lace, under a close-fitting puce jacket that matches her cap.

Parting Kiss

Decamps gave this little girl of 1900 long chestnut brown ringlets that surrond her matte porcelain face, with open mouth, two rows of teeth, large blue eyes, and painted eyelashes. She waves her left hand in a parting gesture and holds a lace-bordered handkerchief in her right. Her far-off expression seems to dwell on the person who received her parting kiss. Dressed in dark rose satin, she evokes the fashion of the end of the nineteenth century. Her fingers, molded in lacquered cardboard, are affectionately separated.

Gavrochinette

"Put a fifty-centime piece in the slot, and Gavrochinette will whistle you a tune": that is the legend on the brass plate fixed to the base of this mechanical doll. Indeed, the young lady hollows her cheeks, rounds her lips, and really does whistle. She winks with one eye, then the other, and her chest rises when she takes in air. She knows six different melodies with complex modulations, trills, and runs. The mechanism, created by Phalibois in Paris, 1900, deserves close examination. No recording of this quality could have come down to us from that period, and the whistler has lasted nearly one hundred years. Its secret is the flute, as old as antiquity. Skin bellows, found in bagpipes, have been used to send air into flutes for centuries; this is the system employed in

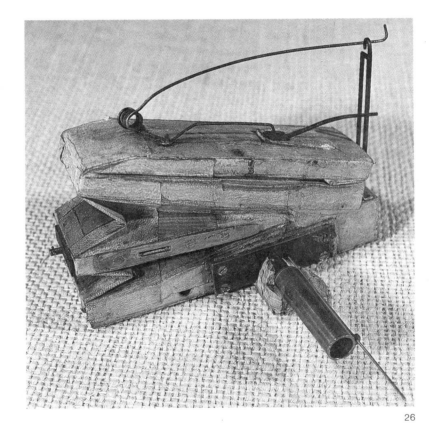

26

the organ. But organ pipes each have a fixed dimension and a single note. Jaquet-Droz, the most skillful of mechanical doll constructors, had the idea of replacing organ pipes with a single acoustic pipe in which a moving piston varied the tonality. Miniaturization then became possible. Gavrochinette is equipped with this mechanism. The accompanying photograph 26, page 30, shows the bellows and, underneath, the acoustic tube in which the piston moves. A little stem along the piston governs the arrival of air and thus modulates its time. The bellows is also a marvel of ingenuity. It has three double-acting compartments controlled by a crank arm, driven in turn by an eccentric gear. The crank arm pumps air in and out of the third compartment, which expands until a calibrated skin valve limits the pressure to the right size. Thus air flows evenly through the whistle, producing a continuous sound. Thanks to the complex cams and a lever (28) that acts on the valve, the arriving air can be interrupted to follow the chosen melody. An additional smaller cam acts on the piston and modulates the sound. At the end of each tune, a device causes the cams to change their "fingering," and the next tune begins. At the end of the series, the mechanism returns to zero.

28

30

34

Barrister

Standing behind his rostrum, dressed in a black robe
with a white pleated frill, this barrister with his abundant
hair, with moustache, and monocle in his left eye, casts
an impressive glance over his audience before
indulging in grand arm gestures. He tilts his head
forward, lowers his eyelids, then lifts his head up slowly
and opens his mouth wide, looking right and left at the
assembly. All these movements take place to an
acrimonious tune produced by a musical cylinder
and comb.

32

The mechanism that allows him to use so many
gestures to punctuate his speech is complex. Hidden
behind his desk, at its base, are seven wooden cams
aligned along same shaft, each cam with ten or twenty

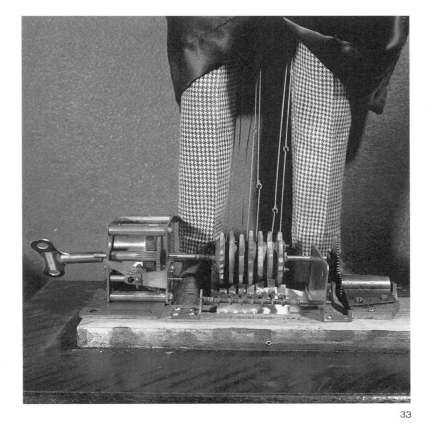

33

lugs (33). For each turn of the cam shaft, nearly one hundred different positions are possible for the various mobile parts of the figure.

34

Little Girl Crying

This little girl, made by Lambert in 1890, is an animated doll rather than a real automaton with complex mechanism and several movements. She contemplates despairingly her broken punchinello puppet, lifts its arm with its string to examine it, turns her head, that lays it down, wiping her tears with a fine embroidered lace handkerchief held in her left hand. Her delicate, expressive head is of biscuit ware and her tears are glass beads. These little automatic dolls, made in great number by Lambert, were dressed by his wife, Madame Lambert-Bourgeoise, a couturière who took up doll dressmaking. Her name was associated with her husband's through the intials L. B. molded in bronze on the keys that operated the clockwork. This doll still wears its original flounced satin dress, decorated at the hem with spangles and sequins.

continued from page 7

This amusement was evidently of an uncertain taste, but widespread in Europe at that time. Even at the château of Hellbrunn, which Marcus Sitticus, archbishop of Salzburg, built at the beginning of the seventeenth century close to the gates of his town, a visitor can find these intemperate water games, in different forms and in several different places. Furthermore, the château boasts in perfect working order the complete panoply of hydraulic marvels that were the pride of princely châteaux of the times. In one grotto, at the foot of a statue of Neptune, the *germaul,* or "yawning mouth," rolls its eyes and sticks out its tongue at visitors as soon as a little container hidden in its jaws fills with water. In other grottoes relatively simple mechanisms permit us to hear remarkably imitated birdsong, to see Apollo flaying Marsyas, or to watch Perseus fighting the sea monster. But the central wonder of the garden at Hellbrunn is perhaps its mechanical theater. About 1750, Lorenz Rosenegger reconstructed in a barrel-valuted niche a quarter of the little baroque town with its trades and social classes: a butcher slaughters a calf in the street, musicians play, Hungarian gypsies dance with a bear, soldiers stand guard before the town hall. All these figure are animated by the original hydraulic mechanism, which also operates an organ that plays a chorale. Also in working order in many European towns are the well-known automatons called Jacquemards, which originated in the Middle Ages. The earliest examples are found in churches. The Catholic Church, in fact, first had the idea of using the fascination exercised by these mechanical dolls as a means of attracting followers and leading them to the true faith. Just as it encouraged religious theater, so the church utilized automatons in lively and evocative shows to present pious figures and picturesque episodes from the Old and New Testaments. These animated statues incarnating prophets, saints, and apostles were driven by mechanical clocks, the finest of which is the astronomical clock at the cathedral of Strasbourg. Often in these great clocks, the hour is struck by a figure with a hammer, who is called the Jacquemard.

But the Jacquemard soon left the church to take up a position in the middle of the town, on a tower summit where it set about its favorite occupation in a secular context. The one at the Samaritaine in Paris, which disappeared in 1813, was famous in its time. The Jacquemard of Dijon, happily preserved, is still well known today. Even more renowned, however, are the two bronze Moors who for almost five centuries have struck the hours in the Clock Tower at Venice, with slow alternating hammerblows, on a bell now rung for the pleasure of tourists gathered in St. Mark's Square.

During this period, in the sixteenth and seventeenth centuries, the two German towns of Nuremberg and Augsburg began to specialize in the manufacture of clockwork figures, animals, and other objects that were marvels of the goldsmith's art. Prized and expensive, these mechanical dolls are exceptional works of art whose animation adds only one more wonder. Made for princes, many were ordered by great eastern lords and used as diplomatic presents.

The finest of these clockwork pieces is perhaps Charles V's ship, exhibited today in the National Renaissance Museum and the château of Ecouen. This extraordinary masterpiece attributed to Hans Schlottheim (1545-1625) was built about 1585, probably at Augsburg. The vessel of gilt brass is mounted on wheels. When the mechanism is started, it advances in a meandering trajectory. An organ plays and trumpeters on the bridge raise their instruments to their lips while drums and cymbals keep time. Cannons sound at regular intervals. On the prow sailors hoist the sails while others on patrol inspect the rear masts and sails. The emperor Charles V is seated on a canopy-covered throne on the poop deck. He lowers his scepter and turns his head while dignitaries circulate around him. At the foot of the main mast is the frame of the pendulum, enameled and with two hands, rare for the sixteenth century. The pendulum sets off two more figures who ring a bell on the hour and each quarter-hour.

This unique work was doubtless meant to serve as a table centerpiece, called a "side-dish," for a meal or gala reception. Great pleasure was taken in watching mechanical dolls during these interminable banquets. Such automatons included table clocks decorated with allegorical figures or fabulous animals – griffins, winged lions, and unicorns; vessels transporting picturesque figures; animated cribs; orchestras composed of musicicians playing various instruments; or mythological scenes, such as the Diana with stag constructed at Augsburg about 1620 by the goldsmith Joachim Fries. In this the last piece, a mechanism in the plinth allowed the figure to move along the festive table while the dogs roused their heads. It was the custom of the times for the guest in front of whom this hunting Diana stopped to remove the stag's head, which served as a cup, fill it, and drink the contents.

The eighteenth century was the great period of the android, the mechanical doll with a human form that imitates human behavior. Two names stand out unquestionably in this domain: Jacques Vaucanson (1709-1782) and the Jaquet-Droz family.

Vaucanson was consumed by a passion for mechanics from his childhood. As a novice with the Minims of Lyon he scandalized the provincial of the order by making mechanical dolls that served him at table. The provincial hastened to destroy these infernal creatures. Consequently abandoning his religiuos life, Vaucanson went on to study anatomy, music, and mechanics at Paris before beginning in 1735, at the age of twenty-six, the construction of three celebrated mechanical dolls that made him famous throughout Europe. Voltaire called him "the rival of Prometheus." Paralleling his activity as mechanician, Vaucanson proved to be as ingenious an inventor. We owe to him the invention of the rubber pipe and the machine that automatically weaves brocaded fabric, erroneously attributed to Jacquard.

What did these celebrated mechanical dolls represent, and what made Vaucanson famous? The answer relies on contemporary documents, since the androids are lost today. Two are described for us in a prospectus probably written by Vaucanson himself. The first android was "a life-size man dressed as a savage who plays eleven tunes on the flute with the same movements of his lips and fingers, and with breath from his mouth like a living man." The *flute player* was effectively exhibited at Paris in the spring of 1738, and many curious viewers came to admire "this masterpiece of the human mind." To dispel the skepticism of his critics, Vaucanson presented a paper to the Academy of Sciences, which validated the invention through the arbitration of its permanent secretary, Fontenelle, in these terms:

"Having heard the reading of a paper by Mr. de Vaucanson concerning the description of a statue in wood copied from the fawn of Coysevox, which plays twelve different tunes on the flute with a precision that has merited public attention and which has been witnessed by a large part of the Academy, the Academy has judged that this machine is extremely ingenious. The author has been obliged to use new simple methods in giving to the finger of the figure the movements necessary to modify the wind which enters the flute, by increasing or diminishing the speed according to the different tunes, by varying the disposition of the lips, and by the movement of a valve which takes on the functions of the tongue. Finally, in imitating through his art all that man is obliged to do and more besides, and in presenting a paper of a clarity and precision rivaling that of his machine, Mr. de Vaucanson has proved his intelligence and his great knowledge of the different elements of mechanics."

The second mechanical doll, also perfected by Vaucanson in 1738, was "a life-size man dressed as a Provençal shepherd, which plays with all the precision and perfection of a skillful player twenty different tunes on a small Provençal flute with one hand, and a tambourine with the other."

The third doll, paradoxically, was not an android but a duck, without doubt the most famous mechanical doll in the world. This remarkable artificial creature of gilt brass could drink, eat, crow, and splash in water, and had the digestion of a living duck. A detailed description of the working of this famed duck has been left by a journalist: "The bird raises its head, looks all around, wags its tail, stretches itself out, spreads out its wings and flaps them while letting out a really natural cry as if it were going to fly away. The effect is even more surprising when the winged creature, leaning toward its plate, starts to swallow the grain with incredibly realistic movements.... As for its digestive system, nobody has managed to explain it."

On this last point the great illusionist Robert Houdin, who saw the duck exhibited at Paris in 1844, gives an interesting explanation:

"The animal was presented with a vessel that held grain soaked in water. The pecking movement made by the beak separated the food and facilitated its introduction into a pipe placed under the lower beak of the duck; water and grain thus ingested fell into a box placed under the stomach of the mechanical doll, and the box was emptied every two or three performances. The evacuation was prepared in advance. A pulp composed of green bread crumbs was pushed by a pump and carefully received on a silver plate as the product of an artificial digestion."

Although today we have lost all trace of these three mechanical dolls that made Vaucanson famous, we can still admire in the Museum of Neuchâtel the three celebrated androids created by the Jacquet-Droz family. The father, Pierre Jacquet-Droz, was born at La Chaux-de-Fonds in 1721, to a family of clockmakers. Like Vaucanson, after a first attraction to the religious life he opted for mechanics. About 1770, with his son Henri-Louis and his mechanician Jean-Frédéric Leschot, he created and made three mechanical dolls that assured the survival of this name: a writer, a harpsichord player, and an artist.

For more than a century these androids traveled Europe. They were presented to the public in return for an entrance fee and advertised by posters describing these marvels of clockwork technology. Thus in 1789 at Paris it was possible "for twenty-four sols each" to see "several musical mechanical dolls invented and programmed by Mr. Jaquet-Droz the younger from Neuchâtel, Switzerland, and executed by Mr. Leschot, mechanician."

The *harpsichord player* was "a figure representing a girl of ten or twelve, who touches a real harpsichord. This mechanical doll, whose body, head, eyes, legs, and fingers make many natural movements, with great precision executes by itself several pieces of music on the harpsichord. Its head and eyes are completely mobile. It looks alternately at the music and at its fingers. At the end of each tune, it curtsies to the audience by an inclination of the body and a movement of the head. Its throat rises and lowers alternately, and so regularly that one might believe it was breathing."

A detailed description of the writer and the artist can be found in a newspaper, the *Diable Boiteux*, of October 15, 1923. The article invites readers to come and ad- *continued on page 64*

36

37

The Painter Poet

This large mechanical doll (90 cm) created by Vichy in Paris (1875) is one of the most interesting in the collection, revealing at each instant an extraordinary animated detail.

To begin with, his eyes wide open, he looks around him for a sujbect (38), then bends over his drawing pad and starts to sketch, raising his head frequently to take in the features of his model. He screws up his eyes to get a better view, moves his hips, raises the strap on his quiver of paint brushes and continues his work (40). When at last he believes that he has arrived at a likeness, he stops a moment, puts aside his pencil, and presents his achievement (39), the portrait of someone in the audience (36). And suddenly this portrait comes to life, laughs derisively, and acknowledges the latter's reaction by wagging its jaw and making its hat dance on its head. The powerful mechanism (37) is contained in the chair on which the painter is seated. Two cam shafts turning at different speeds are necessary to carry out all the complex movements.

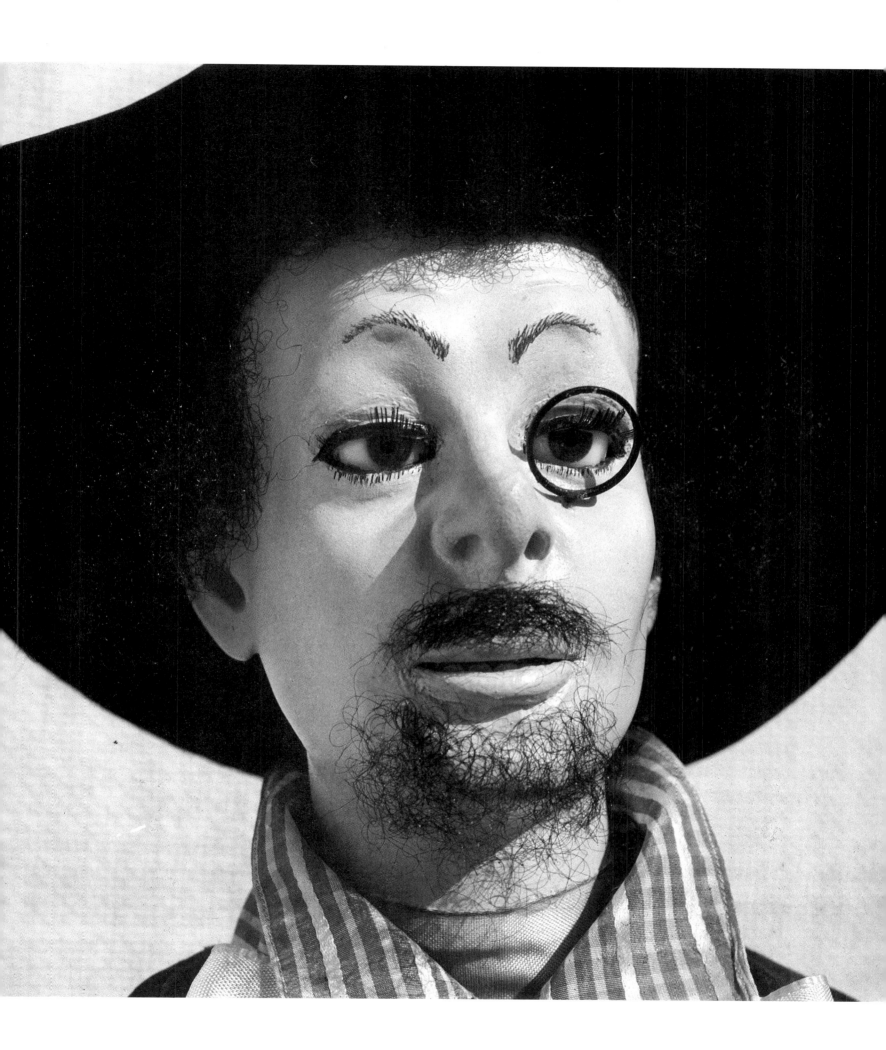

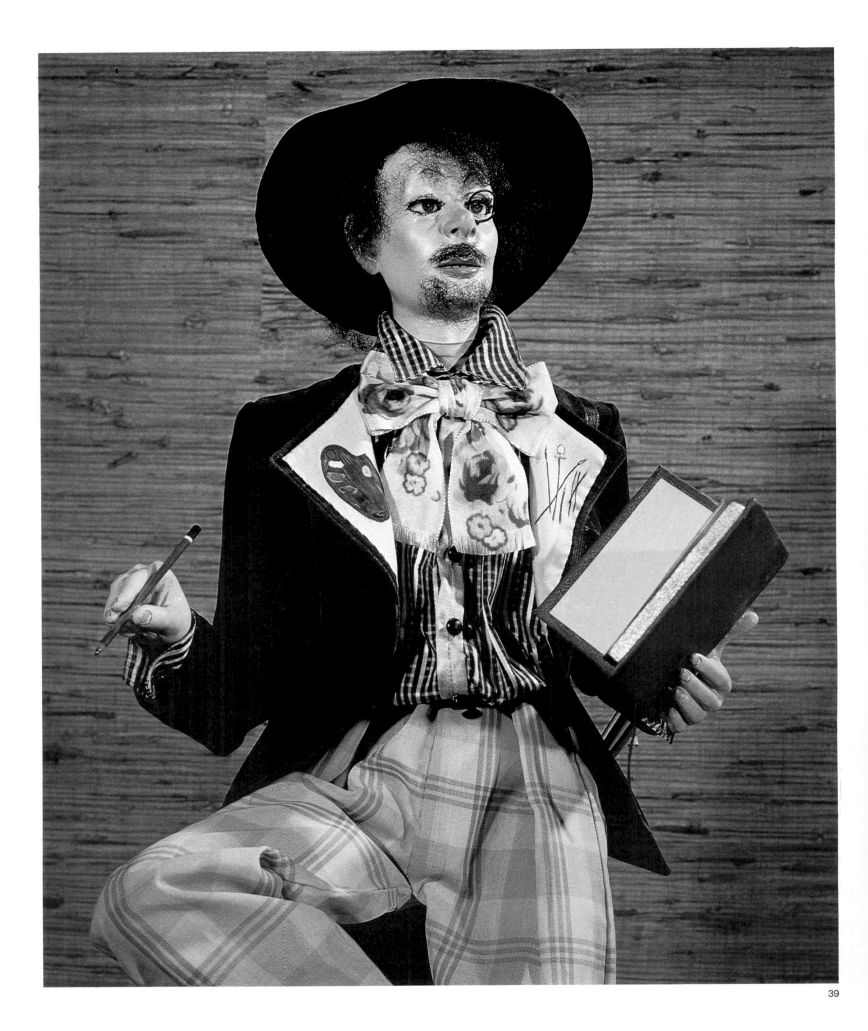

Washerwoman

This washerwoman by Decamps, Paris, 1900, with head and forearms of biscuit ware, stands behind a tub placed on a tripod. In her right hand she holds a brush that she passes through the palm of her left hand, which once held a piece of soap whose place of attachment is still visible. She moves her head backward and forward. Her long hair, partly hidden under an organdy bonnet, frames a face with blue eyes and an open mouth revealing two rows of teeth. Under her red and white vertically striped skirt, the washerwoman wears cotton socks with fine horizontal stripes. Her pointed sabots are of beige glove leather, and she washes her clothes to the sprightly air of "The Bells of Corneville."

Young Lady with Parasol

This young lady with a biscuit-ware doll's head is exceptionally tall (1.2 m.). Standing on her base, she turns her head right and left and lifts a parasol with her right hand. Her left hand slightly raises the bottom of her pink taffeta dress, under which appears a white petticoat sewn at the hem to a rigid framework.

Painter and Sculptor

These two monkeys by Phalibois, 1870, are certainly gentlemen, as their clothes would indicate. The sound of a sculotor's hammer hitting a chisel resounds through the pane of this animated scene. On the block of pure marble worked by the sculptor appears a woman's silhouette, rounded with several draperies. The painter makes rapid brushstrokes. All around, in the bohemian disorder of the atelier, are paint boxes, tools, sketches, and cardboard. But the impressive miniature machinery that gives life to this large scene (80 by 95 cm. high) is invisible.

The movement is produced by a longitudinal shaft carrying fourteen cams. The cams govern wires that pass through each leg of the monkeys and move their limbs. So complicated are the trajectories from the levers controlling the movements that the constructor had to relay the wire with fishline, today more than one hundred years old.

44

45

Pierrot with Dogs

This fairly big automaton (90 cm. high), created by Vichy in Paris, 1865, belongs to the large family of circus subjects popular at the period. The mechanism is concealed in the box under the trestle, among the artist's accessories (48). A little black dog turns round and round on his pedestal before, after several hesistations, jumping through the hoop held out by Pierrot. All the ingenuity of the eighteenth-century constructors is apparent in this mechanical doll. Not only is the subject in general rich with inventive details, but a touch of magic has been added: how does the dog pass through the hoop, which seems completely filled in? Pierrot's face, particularly delicate, is made of molded papier-mâché, covered with a hard tinted glaze and painted according to the client's wishes (47). Successful mechanical doll were reproduced several times, but each one differed in decoration, clothing, and accessories. The hands (50) are in the same material as the head, and the eyelids are mobile.

48

49

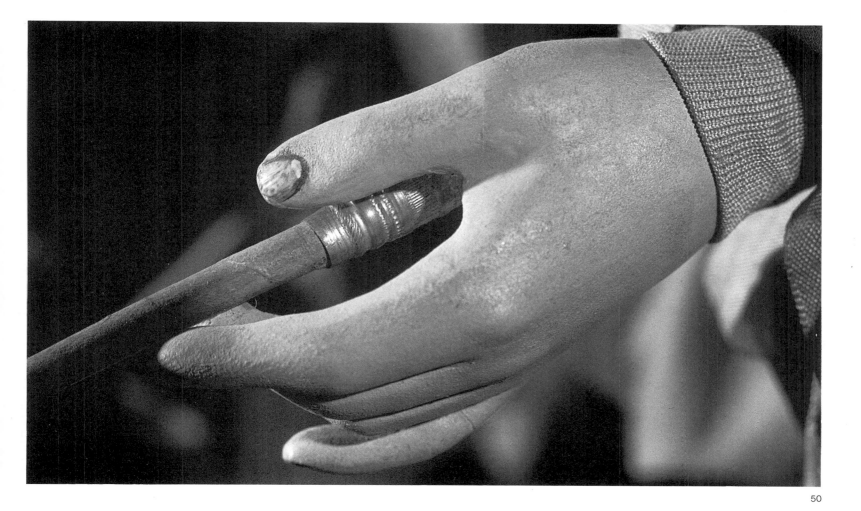

50

Pierrot Writing

This writing Pierrot by Lambert, 1875, is of a moderate size, sixty-four centimeters high. He is seated before a table where he writes to Columbine. From time to time he stretches out his left arm to rekindle the flame of a lamp, the intensity of which varies. It is a real oil lamp with an ingenious mechanism that winds the wick up and down, changing its luminosity. He writes with a goose's feather, using his right hand, and his letter is visible (54). While he writes, he leans his head toward the paper, raising it from time to time to think or to adjust the wick of the lamp. The mechanism is lodged in the body itself (53) and is wound up by means of a removable key, whose keyhole is concealed beneath the tail of his tunic. Five cams are mounted on the cylinder shaft, but with the aid of bell-crank levers and steering devices, ten different movements are possible. The success of this mechanical doll is not only due to its delicate execution and graceful features, but also to its true-to-life gestures. Indeed, careful examination of the configuration of its skeleton reveals that it is based on the human structure, with an identical orientation of the axes of articulation (55). Only six examples of this mechanical doll are known today. Curiously, the music that accompanies it is not Lully's well-known "Au Clair de la Lune," but a charming little air that has not been identified.

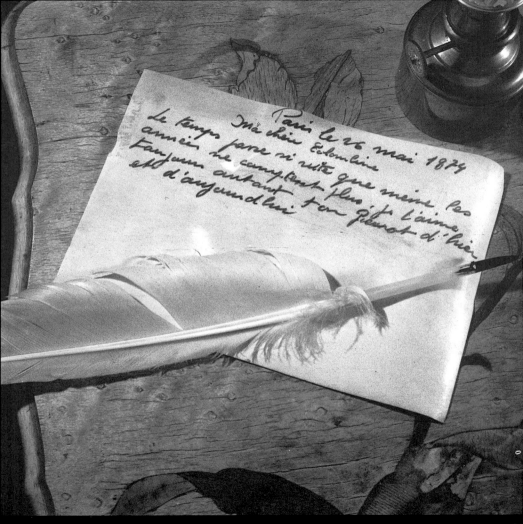

Paris le 26 mai 1874

Ma chère Colombine

Le temps passe si vite que même les
années ne comptent plus si je t'aime
toujours autant, ton Pierrot d'hier
est d'aujourd'hui

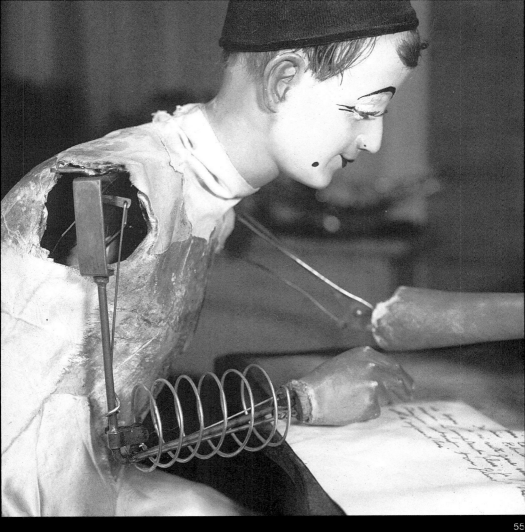

Clown with Parasol

This figure by Vichy, 1878, rolls a ball on the edge of a fan, which he shakes with his left hand. At the same times he looks all around to seek applause and flutters his eyelashes in false modesty. He twirls a parasol with his right hand, balancing a revolving porcelain plate on its edge. The moon that decorates his costume also opens animated eyelids. The spring-driven mechanism is placed in the base and wires run through the legs. Head and hands are of paper-mâché, and the music is produced by a cylinder and comb.

continued from page 43 mire the androids of the Jacquet-Droz family, newly presented at Paris:

"Come to the rue du Richelieu, at its corner with the boulevard Montmartre, and you will see there a child of brass, cardboard, and wood, to whom you can dictate what you like. Obedient, it will trace for you with its pen in the most elegant letters the word or phrase you have requested.... Although its intellect is organized on springs and it is habituated to a rectitude of movement determined in advance by the master who gives it its quarter-hour of existence by means of a key thrust into its back, we certify that this child has more intelligence than is needed to be the secretary of an adult. We certify this all the more strongly knowing that this is foolishness, even if it writes all that is dictated to it, because it is built for that purpose, because its life is the life of a slave and its brain, soul and heart, a brain, soul, and heart of bronze.

"Beside this young "general" secretary (because it writes for everybody) there is another child, even more generous than the first. This one has all the independence of the artist it imitates. We admit that the mechanical merit of this child, or rather of its few minutes of life, is something far more admirable than easy to describe. It seems that a divine breath animates it all during the time in which it finishes its drawing, which it sketches out completely and then fills in before us with a crayon. It is impossible to conceive of the delicacy of its hand. Its drawing has not the simple and regular line of a machine; one senses the already skilled crayon of a young artist. It draws in precise places, guiding its hand with such subtlety and delicacy that we doubt if any artist could execute more quickly or clearly an imagined sketch.... During its work its eyes follow its crayon. It seems to ponder from time to time, to retrace the strokes not sufficiently marked, to move from one place to another with a grace that arouses envy among those onlookers who would like to do as well as "he." It is even seen to blow on the paper when something gets in the way of its crayon."

One might continue to describe other famous mechanical dolls constructed at the end of the eighteenth and early nineteenth century, from the tympanum player of Pierre Kintzing and David Roentgen to the artists and magicians of the Maillardet family, from the musicians of Friedrich von Knaus to the mechanical animals and clocks of James Cox, as well as the musical dolls of the Kaufmann family. The brevity of this historical summary, necessarily incomplete, has only permitted mention of some of these masterpieces of clockwork mechanics and their constructors.

The extreme complexity of the mechanism of these mechanical dolls and the thousands of hours of work needed to make them, to create really unique pieces, meant that their constructors were forced either to sell them to enthusiasts at high prices or to exibit them to a paying public. The number of purchasers rich enough to afford such costly pieces rapidly diminished at the beginning of the nineteenth century. But at the same time the desire for mechanical dolls spread to a wider public, which acquired animated figures, animals, and other objects as toys for children or, more often, for adults.

"Man is only really man when he is at play," wrote Schiller. In this sense the middle classes of the last century demonstrated a particularly well-developed sense of humanity. In response to these demands a mechanical doll industry sprang up, principally at Paris. The situation must not be misunderstood, however. If the automatons created by the Lambert family, Vichy, Deschamps, Roullet, and others, were no longer unique inventions, each of them was conceived and produced with meticulous care and attention and even the most popular subjects were made in small numbers.

As the decades passed, the progressive disappearance of many nineteenth-century mechanical dolls made those that survived increasingly rare. Due to their beauty, the quality of their workmanship, and eventually their scarcity, these dolls are sought today by museums and collectors ready to pay a small fortune to acquire them. Madeleine de Galéa collected more than ninety of these mechanical dolls throughout her life, and her collection is of exceptional interest to an ever-growing worldwide public.

Antoine Battaini
Directeur des Affaires culturelles
of the Principality

58

59

60

Acrobat with Ladder

This large figure (1.1 m. high), with a taut body and head held high, was made by Vichy in 1875. He begins his act by taking hold of a ladder with both hands, then, slightly rocking it to find his balance, lifts himself upside-down, as straight as a tree. His movement is remarkable because he is perched on top of the ladder, which he oscillates to keep his balance. But the exploit becomes stupefying when he proceeds to let go with one hand. When we see such prowess it is easy to understand why mechanical dolls are so fascinating: even with modern techinques such a construction would be extraordinary. His features are delicate and his stage costume sumptuous. His hands and face were especially created for this work, of papier-mâché covered with gutta-percha and ivorine.

Clown with Stilts

This acrobat (80 cm. high) pretends to be drunk and reels backward and forward after taking a swig right from the bottle. The mechanism is remarkable: all the functions are conveyed inside the right stilt and join a relaying apparatus situated in the body. This apparatus permits him to raise and swing the left stilt, leaving him balanced on one. The period music is produced by a cylinder and comb.

62

63

Dancing Countryman

Dressed in his Sunday clothes, he sways with a rolling
gait, balances with one leg back and forwards,
swings his arms, and nods his head to the rhythm
of a little tune.

64

Oriental Dancer

The real feat of this dancer is hidden. A single brass cam works two wires that pass through one leg. Thus, with its twelve lugs, this single cam lasciviously undulates the dancer in a suggestive dance. The first wire turns the body around an oblique axis, producing the swaying of the hips and the movements of the bust, while arms and head move in the other direction because they are attached by cords to fixed points.

The Galéa Collection

All who had the privilege of knowing the collection of Madeleine de Galéa in the setting she developed for it over the years guard the memory of a marvelous world in which hundreds of dolls and dozens of mechanical dolls brought their period to life. Access to this enchanted world was reserved for the privileged few who, during a visit to the collector, rediscovered the spirit of childhood, through these artifacts created by the imaginations of able technicians.

This volume is devoted exclusively to the mechanical dolls in the Galéa collection, all of which were produced in France during the second half of the nineteenth century. They thus represent many of the subjects in fashion at that time, recalling the preferences and interests of those alive then. Are they drawing-room objects or adult's toys? We do not know exactly. The only certitude is that they were brought together by a collector passionately attracted by all survivals of the nineteenth century.

Before turning in detail to the dolls themselves, let us consider the origin of this astonishing collection, the fruit of a lifetime's enthusiastic quest. Madeleine Morau was born at Réunion, a French island in the Indian Ocean, in 1874. As a young girl, she moved with her mother to Paris. Their search for a house brought them to the neighborhood of Auteuil, where they discovered the villa that fulfilled their aspirations. Unhappy to have left behind the mild skies of her island, the small and rather melancholy girl brought with her the dolls that were her childhood companions. Her mother, to soften the blow of a move perhaps rather severe for a child, continued to offer her new dolls. Where better than in Paris could one find these "Parisiennes," fashionable dolls that would become a real passion for the young woman? As an adult, she never ceased to surround herself with dolls, whose porcelain heads and fixed expressions are so strangely seductive.

Her glamorous life in Paris, amid many artists, led her to meet a young diplomat to Russia, Edmond de Galéa, whom she wed. Among the couple's friends were well-known painters. Madeleine de Galéa posed at different times in her life for Renoir and Bonnard, to name only two. Nor to be forgotten is the sympathy that bound the couple to Ambroise Vollard, whom she had known as a child on Réunion. As an uprooted young man, he found a friendly reception in their home when he arrived in Paris from the island, like a fish out of the water. Vollard was the editor of Chagall, Bonnard, Rouault, and others. So enthusiastic and well-informed a connoisseur could not have left his friends on the fringe of the artistic world then evolving.

Madeleine de Galéa found herself widowed at an early age. She brought up her son alone, devoting all her spare time to building her collection of dolls. The collection became so large that she was one day obliged to seek a shelter especially for it. Thus she acquired the villa that would be reserved uniquely for her innumerable family with porcelain faces. She gave life to her collection as a whole by arranging the dolls amid miniatures that also evoked daily life in the ninetheenth century. Mme. de Galéa gathered her dolls without any concern for technical or scientific order, but on impulse, simply because she imagined how a doll might take its place in the scenes composed in her imagination. Was she seduced by an expression or the train of a crinoline dress with a bustle, and a hat trimmed with ostrich feathers or flowers? The motivation is unimportant. She let herself be guided by the detail that charmed her.

The visitor can appreciate the refinement and taste of

Madeleine de Galéa by Renoir   66

the collector in the miniature furniture made by master craftsmen, the many doll-size services in Parisian porcelain, and the thousand tiny everyday objects that give such atmosphere to the collection. The some four hundred dolls themselves are dressed in contemporary costume and constitute a remarkable document on the fashions of the times. Corsets, gaiters, countless petticoats with pleated or embroidered skirts, socks and openwork stockings, and miniature powder compacts and gloves, not to mention hats, completed outfits for every hour of the day. All the luxury and refinement of the period can be found in this miniature world.

But perhaps all these dolls, motionless in their luxurious settings, became tedious to her. One day she turned her interest and affection to those strange figures, occasionally grotesque, that move with the turn of a key, accompanied by a music-box tune, amazing the spectators. Their creators never suspected how, several decades later, cinema and television would invade daily life, creating a miniaturized animation that had once seemed possible for mechanical dolls alone.

In this fascirating world, Christian de Galéa, grandson of the collector, grew up, raised by a grandmother who took on the role when his mother was prematurely divided from her infant son. Madeleine de Galéa was as attentive to the education of her grandson as she was faithful to her passion for dolls and automatons. He distinguished himself, among other things, as a brilliant tennis player. In his honor, she created the Galéa Cup, an award to encourage young sportsmen. André de Feuquières, in *My Paris and...*, conjures precisely the fragile silhouette of Mme. de Galéa:

"Madame de Galéa, stopping off at Auteil near the curious house of Hortense Schneider on the Avenue de Versailles, had all the lightly languid grace of those young ladies raised under mild and enchanting skies.... The last time I had seen her was a long time ago. It was at Deauville where she presented the winner's cup to a tennis champion and I remember her smile and gesture. She like to dress herself in vaporous materials and I could only think of her today clouded in tulle and muslin. This taste for fragile and delicate finery accounted, no doubt, for much in the charming collection that she engendered and that soon took on the proportions of a real museum. Dolls from every country and from every age looked at you, severely, mockingly, or tenderly from one end to another of Madame de Galéa's mansion. These precious people seemed to find fault with your appearance, your size, your clumsy intrusion into their enchanted universe. It was a bit hallucinatory, but it was not so disagreable."

After the death, in 1956, of this grandmother whom he cherished and admired so much, Christian de Galéa offered the collection to the Principality of Monte Carlo. It found a worthy showcase when H.R.H. Prince Rainier III provided a superb villa typical of the style of Charles Garnier. With its pilasters, garlands, and firepots, the house has all the seductive baroque decoration of the end of the last century, characteristic of the architect of the Operas at Paris and at Montpellier and the opera room in the casino at Monte Carlo. Built as a private residence for the German banker Sauber, the house once had a path from the garden to the sea. After various occupants it was abandoned in the mid-forties, and luxuriating vegetation obliterated every detail of the garden. After some years of neglect the villa came back to life for the Galéa Collection. Its rooms became exhibition spaces for the dolls and automatons painstakingly restored by the chief curator, Gabriel Ollivier. It was he who created the museum and made the collection known, so that today it attracts and charms visitors from all over the world.

Ollivier knew where to find competent artists and specialists to restore the collection so that it would retain its special character, even if the exhibition now is not rigorously that imagined by Madeleine de Galéa. The dolls are again presented in rooms with scale decoration. Visitors can appreciate the evocative costumes of the period, fashioned by the hands of skillfull couturiers, as expert in these miniature costumes as in their designs for human customers.

In the midst of the dolls, the automatons always arouse the curiosity of a wide-ranging public: enthusiasts fascinated with clockwork – a technical skill always needed in the conception of these figures – who can appreciate the technical achievement of such mechanical constructions; adults who dream of another epoch; and children who, although accustomed to technical achievements, are no less attracted by these beings with theatrical masks, arousing emotion, amusement, sympathy, and sometimes apprehension.

In all, more than ninety mechanical dolls of various categories are found in the collection from the stars, with complex functions and detailed modeling, to mechanical dolls cut out of sheet iron, simple mechanical toys. Various degrees of inspiration are shown by the creators. Yet a certain homogeneity appears in the ensemble, and four great names stand out: Decamps, Léopold Lambert (1854-1935), Vichy, and H. Phalibois. All created their figures for the most part between 1855 and the beginning of our century.

Which of the stars deserves the place of honor? The painter-poet (page 44) with blue eyes in a Bohemian costume, showing the drawing that he touches up for spectators amused by his winks and the way he alternately shrugs his shulders? The romantic Pierrot-writer (page 56), who adjusts the flame of his oil lamp to write to Columbine with a hard-wearing goose feather? The snake-charmer (page 24)? Her delicately modeled body reflects Decamp's new conception of the automaton: "A mechanical doll is moving sculpture." Only a sculptor sensitive to the fresh sensuality of female beauty could convey such corporal elegance, the sympathetic magic of the green blue eyes that filters through mobile eyelids to charm the snake. Or the acrobat with ladder (page 66), who, when placed on the top of his ladder, leaves the spectator astonished by the complexity of his wiring, which enables him to let go of the ladder with his right hand after turning a half-circle over the void? The acrobatic performance apart, the clown is captivating with the delicacy of his painted features and hands precisely sculpted in papier-mâché. Most of these figures can be classed in categories corresponding to certain period interests. For example, the clown belongs to a circus series immensely popular during the first half of the nineteenth century. Many other clowns are also in the collection: clown acrobats with parasols, a clown with a diabolo game, an illusionist whose head disappears behind a fan and reappears in a cube beside him. A charming Pierrot with performing dogs also belongs to this series, as does a magician formerly part of the decoration of a clock.

The taste for the exotic that inspired such dancers as Loie Fuller appears in the charming animated Japanese continued on page 86

68

69

Acrobats

These clowns execute a hand-to-hand act demanding such an iron constitution that the upper clown one day broke his collarbone (70).

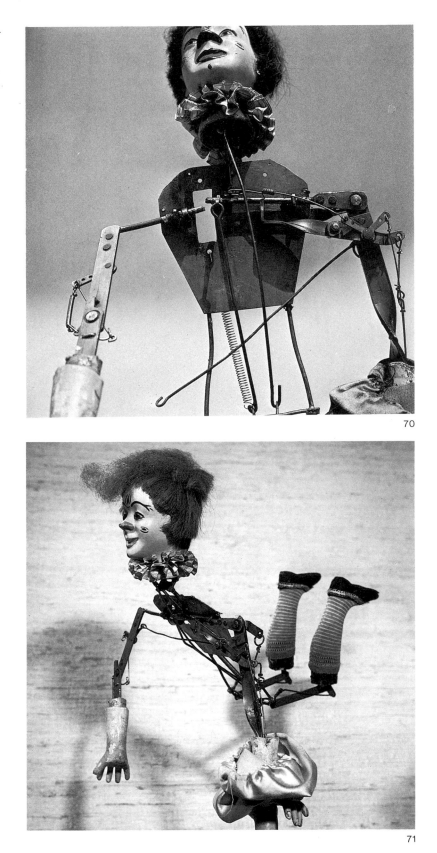

70

71

The joint repaired (71), he now throws himself into
the air again with the aid of his carrier, to a little
tune produced by a cylinder and comb. By Decamps,
the clown and their music date from 1880.

Clown Playing Diabolo

In that large family of the circus, this clown by Vichy,
1895, is a star, with a profoundly human expression

74

76

75

beneath his makeup and a life- size head. He plays diabolo, a game much in fashion at the end of the last century, making him one of the rare mechanical dolls to use a completely detached accessory, the hourglass-shaped top of the diabolo game. He leans forward and lifts up his arms alternately to roll the top, which he follows attentively with his eyes, blinking in time with each movement. The mechanism, situated partly in the base, partly in the body, is very powerful. Even using the large geared-down crank (76), it takes a fair amount of strength to wind the spring. Under such great pressure, the metal wears down around the pivots, causing damage to the plates as shown in one photograph (74). The same pillow block after restoration is shown in another.

77

Conjuror

This illusionist by Phalibois, 1885, is ninety-five centimeters high, perched on a pedestal, and dressed and painted as a clown. He holds·a fan decorated with a pretty scene in his left hand, and begins his act to the sound of a little tune. He smiles, blinks a moment, and hides his face for several seconds with the fan. When the fan is moved aside, his head has disappeared! Then, with his right hand, he lifts the lid of a giant die placed beside him, and out comes his head, quite alive, looks around, smiles, and moves its eyes. He closes the lid, masks himself with the fan, draws it aside, and his head reappers in its proper place. The cycle then begins again. If one looks on from the side, it is possible to see the first head topple over (80). The mechanism, divided between the base and the interior of the body, is complex: it must work both heads and produce extensive movements, including the arm gestures. The forces exercised are so great that some of the cams were worn beyond repair and had to be replaced (82).

81

82

continued from page 75 bust created by Vichy about 1870 (page 16). Reposing on a black-enameled plinth decorated with golden Japanese apple blossoms, this oriental beauty perfectly reflects the decorative style of Paris in that period. Other exotics include the series of musicians that remind us to what extent black slaves with a gift of music were sought at the beginning of the century. Whether these automatons play harp, banjo, or drum, they surprise us with the versatility of their articulated fingers. Their fine bearing captures the attention of spectators. To appreciate them fully, no detail of their movement must be neglected.

Another series that flourished abundantly was made up of monkeys in all shapes and aspects. They form a group insofar as they parody human beings. Indeed, monkeys have had that function since their early appearance on painted panels at the beginning of the eighteenth century, and later on hangings, as porcelain, or as gilt bronze furniture motifs.

These remarks and observations by no means establish a complete repertory of nineteenth-century Parisian mechanical dolls, nor even describe those of the Galéa Collection, but are intended to provide an outline. The photographs and accompanying comments in this volume will enable to reader to understand the mysteries of the doll's mechanisms. By these astonishing devices their inventors, constantly concerned with the laws of anatomy, were able to create in their automantons a perfect illusion of life.

Paris was an important center for the creation of mechanical dolls during the last century. Constructors became famous through the realizations of works that became celebrated as soon as they appeared on the market, in a highly competitive climate. But while the rarest examples were produced in small numbers, the same theme was often treated by several inventors. Thus, before a mechanical doll can be attributed to a particular artist, its mechanism must be carefully examined in order to define its precise characteristics and determine what modifications were undertaken later at more or less expert hands. It was a great temptation for the Sunday do-it-yourselfer to restore life to a mechanical doll rescued from a dusty attic, at a time when these objects had not yet aroused the curiosity of enthusiasts in auction rooms or antique shops.

But to renew the mobility of these hundred-years-olds, often crippled with rheumatism, it is not enough to treasure them. A restorer must know their history and learn how they relate to the technical evolution of their times. These facts cannot be ignored. The meticulous restorer will define the exact alloy of a defective piece and attempt to reproduce it, then shape it in its original form so that it can again fulfil its role, contributing to the magic of movement. The real mission of the restorer. whatever the object to which he applies his knowledge

– painting, ceramics, old textiles, or mechanical dolls –
is always guided by a fundamental care for authenticity;
his study leads to better understanding of how the evidence of the past fits into the history of a patrimony.

Before being exhibited in the National Museum of Monte Carlo, the mechanical dolls of the Galéa Collection are restored to their original working orders. A permanent concern for authenticity governs their maintenance, undertaken by André Soriano whose photographs illustrate this volume. These photographs focus attention on the value of these figures, whose charm must not lead us to forget their fragility, nor to overlook their artistic qualities and historical interest.

Annette Bordeau
Secrétaire General du Musée National
de Monaco

Fairground Hercules

This strongman belongs to the tradition of peripatetic
athletes, buffoons, bear exhibitors, and acrobats who
played on street corners in return for small change. He

84

is dressed in an enormous starred and dotted clown's costume, a cravat, and a short jacket. He bends down to grasp from the trestle in front of him an enormous weight marked "20 kg," which he lifts and presents to his public with an outstretched arm. Even more surprising, he balances this exercise with two light feathers that he holds in his hand. Smiling from behind his glasses, he then thanks his public with a wave of his right hand and a nod. His head is especially modeled in papier-mâché glazed with gutta-percha and ivorine. It is mobile and its eyelashes are particularly animated. The mechanism that works this meter-high Hercules by Phalibois, 1880, consists of five cams, each with six to ten lugs. As the forces involved are great – he bends in two at hip level – there is a powerful spring, and the wheels and pinions are of large dimensions. He performs to a tune of the period played on a cylinder and comb triggered by the motor spring.

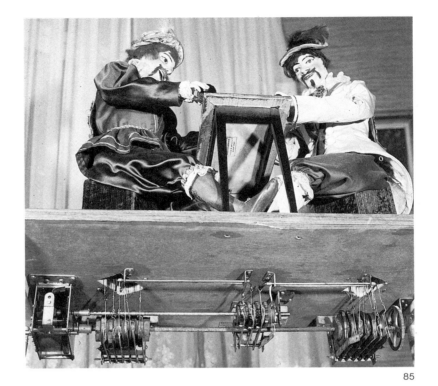

85

Dicers

In a room where the back wall is hung with a carved framed mirror that reflects the backs of two figures, and with two pictures, one by Corot, the other by Gauguin, two dice players face one another. Their chins and mouths are mobile, suggesting animated conversation. Their eyelashes, also mobile, shade two pairs of brown eyes. They seem to take the spectator into their confidence before bending their heads toward the table to see what number has come up on the dice, which one of the players has shaken from a black bowl. With his other hand, the player sweeps clean the table, making the dice fall into the bowl, and then plays again. As the photograph shows (85), the mechanism hidden under the floor is composed of a forest of wires, cams, bell-crank levers, and springs, all needed so that the dice can be thrown freely onto the table, then returned to the bowl. Phalibois created this automaton in 1880, and has given his players trick dice on which the number six appears rather more frequently than it should.

86

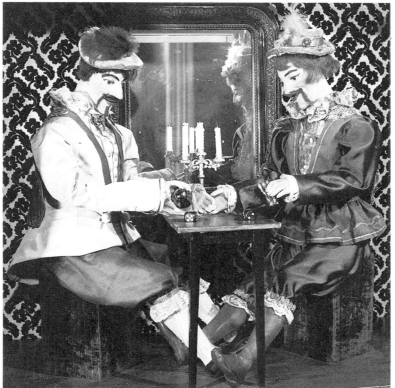

87

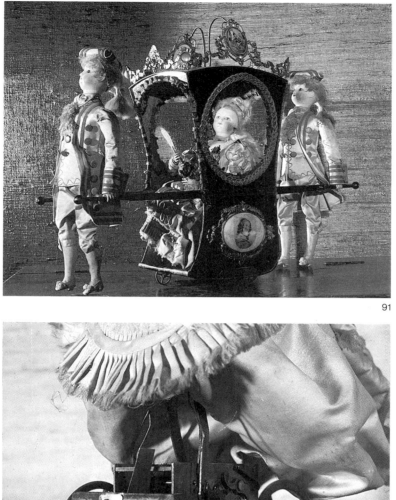

91

92

Sedan Chair Group

Two footmen with wigs, dressed in French style, carry a chair mounted on three wheels, in wich a fashionable woman sits and fans herself to music. She turns her head right and left to look outside, while the porters, with biscuit-ware heads like the lady's, swing their arms in a walking movement. The upper part of the chair is decorated with a gilt bronze cornice of knotted ribbons and flounces embellished with gray pearls and two oval medallions. The rich decoration contributes much to the charm of this mechanical doll, made in 1865 by Vichy. The music is original: two tunes, "The Bird of Paradise" and "The Hunting of the Princes."

93

Pasha Smoking a Hookah

Infatuation with the exotic was rife at the end of the
nineteenth century when Lambert conceived this
smoking pasha. He sits on a base enclosing the
mechanism, with a cup of coffee in his left hand, the tip
of the hookah in his right. He raises them alternately to
his lips in the most delicate manner. Relaxed, almost
blissful, he lifts his head from time to time to exhale the
smoke and half closes his eyes to savor its fragrance.

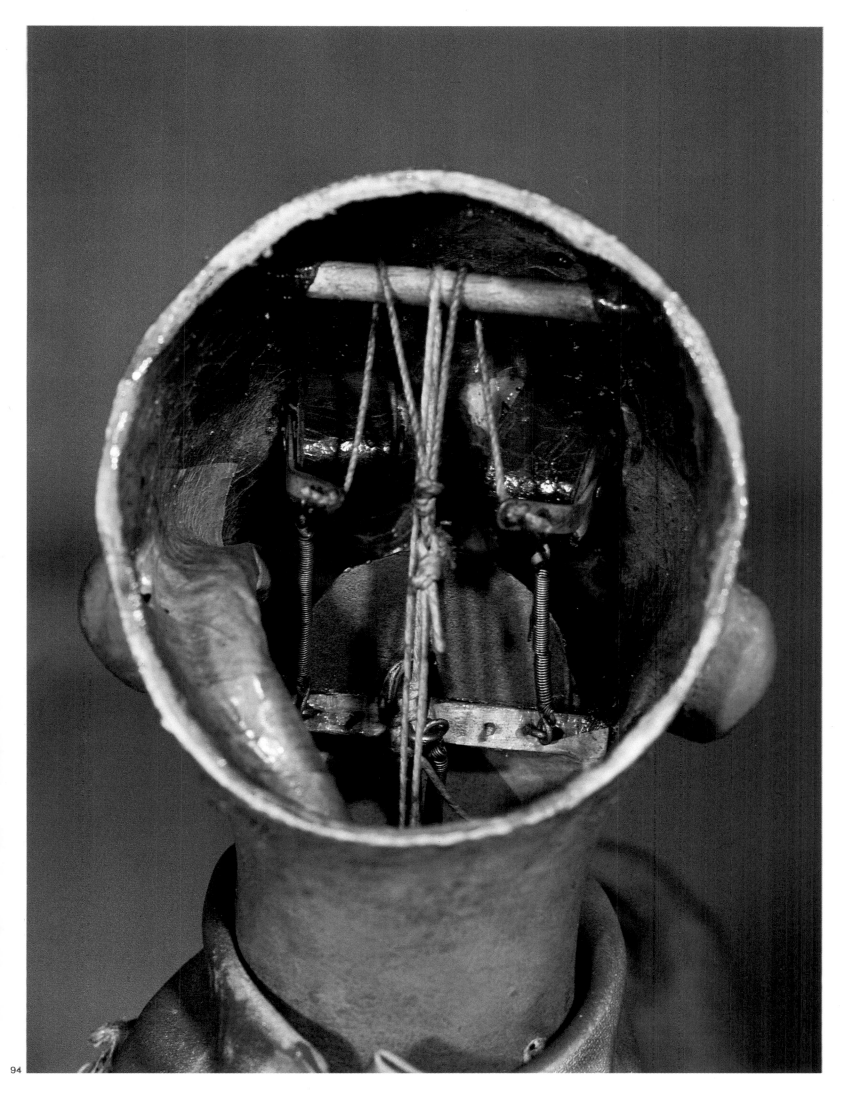

95

To make this mechanical doll function, one first fills the
hookah with pipe tobacco, starts the mechanism to
create the aspiration and lights the tobacco. Very soon
the smoker blows smoke from his mouth and
expresses his satisfaction (95). But how does it work?
On one of the wheels of the mechanism, a little crank
arm of piano cord is worked by an eccentric crank pin.
The crank arm governs the opening and closing of a
sheepskin bellows that, upon opening, inhales smoke
from the pipe bowl. Then the mechanism closes a brass
valve over the tube, and opens the valve of a pipe that

crosses the body to the head, while the bellows dilates, compressing the smoke towards the mouth (98). The pure rubber tubes originally used hardened very quickly, since vulcanization had only recently been invented at this period. No longer flexible and blocked with nicotine, the tube ceased to function correctly and finally broke. Paradoxically, this mishap saved these mechanical dolls, because the mechanism was protected from further wear. After restoration, working as well as they ever did, they continue to breathe their sweet-smelling smoke.

97

98

Hookah Smoker

Every large collection of mechanical dolls was bound to
contain a hookah smoker. So a number of them still
remain, scattered around the world. The smoker always
takes the same posture, seated, alternately drinking
from his cup of coffee and drawing on his hookah. The
hookah may vary in form, like the size of the turban, but,
in every version, he has removed his turkish slippers in
order to be more at ease. The mechanism is always
situated in the back of the base, beside the bellows that
inhales and forces back the smoke. In this example, the
tube of the bellows is artificial; the real duct for the
smoke passes through the hand and arm before
rejoining the bellows, from where it leads off to the
head. This mechanical doll by Lambert is only
moderately tall (58 cm. high); its body is papier-mâché
and its head is is lacquered cardboard.

Smoker with Monocle

This dandy, by Vichy in 1865, wears a suit, white
waistcoat, and a shirt with a pleated dickey embellished
by a loosely tied bow. From time to time he raises his
cigarette holder to his lips and, blinking, expels smoke
through a half-opened mouth. A monocle in his eye, he
then looks to see what effect he has had on his
audience, and starts to smoke again. The mechanism,
which is entirely contained in the body, includes, as with
all the smokers, a sheepskin bellows fitted with valves.
It inhales the smoke from the cigarette holder by way of
a rubber pipe hidden in the right arm and exhales
through a mouth with a mobile jaw by way of another
rubber pipe.

101

Large Smoking Monkey

This seated monkey by Decamps 1880, is nearly a
meter high and has a head larger than human size. The
head is remarkably expressive. Decamps sculpted the
heads of his dolls himself, often in wood, before
carrying out the papier-mâché molding with its several
coats of glaze. The supplementary leather work

102

of the mobile lips and eyelids is finely executed.
The animal is humorously represented sitting on a cane
chair in a typically quadrumanous posture. He wears a
white waistcoat with cutoff corners, a bow tie, red suit
and top hat, and has a bamboo cane, an indispensible
accessory for the elegant man of his period. The
mechanism is classic, with springs, skin bellows, and a
musical cyclinder and comb.

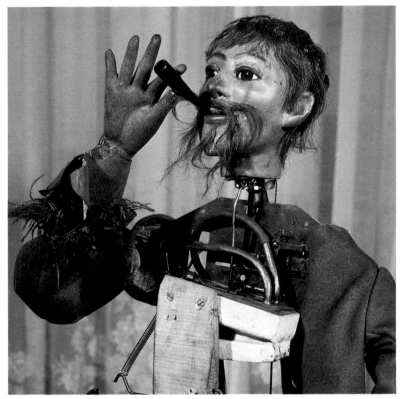

103

Buffalo Bill

The legend of Buffalo Bill, mythical hero of the West, had crossed the Atlantic well before the first steamships. Here he is dressed in his prairie outfit with a wide-brimmed felt hat and his gun near to hand. He takes long drags from the cigarette holder in his right hand (106) without fear of setting fire to his short beard.

104

Then he raises his head, exhaling the smoke. As with all the smokers, his mouth is mobile, facilitating the expulsion of the smoke, which he blows out in little rings. The tubes that line the cigarette holder to the mouth via the bellows became visible at restoration (103). The principle problem of these smoking dolls is the hardening of the rubber tubes due to the tars and other deposits left by the tobacco. Changing them amounts to a real surgical operation (105). First the restorer must remove the stitches from the costume and unglue it, with the greatest caution. Then all the cloth that reinforces the glued parts must be removed, in order to separate the two papier-mâché shells of the body. Also illustrated in the photos (103, 105) are the fishline pulling cords that work the eyelids and lower jaw. The joints of the mouth are concealed beneath the beard and moustache of Buffalo Bill Cody, hero of the National Museum at Monte Carlo.

106

107

Little Smoking Monkey

This attractive little monkey, elegant in his embroidered waistcoat and his top hat, is one of the smallest smoking mechanical dolls, only forty centimeter high without the base. Very agile, he inhales smoke from his cigarette holder and blows is out with a remarkable movement of his lips. Their mobility is due to the fine skin in which they are executed, the same skin used for the eyelids that he half closes to savor the smoke, while balancing on his backside. The mechanism is concealed in the red velvet base. The construction is attributed to Decamps.

109

Conjuring Monkey

The movements of this monkey by Phalibois, 1880, are of an astonishing vivacity because he is an illusionist. He turns his head abruptly, distracting our attention with the rapid gestures of this arms. When he hits the wall on which a picture hangs, it changes subject. Behind the wall, seven scenes dealing with engagements or marriage are painted on a large disk, the mechanism of which the monkey sets off with his sleight-of-hand. Originally, the whole scene must have been under a globe, to judge by the small size of the doll (52 cm. high) and the form of the grooved base.

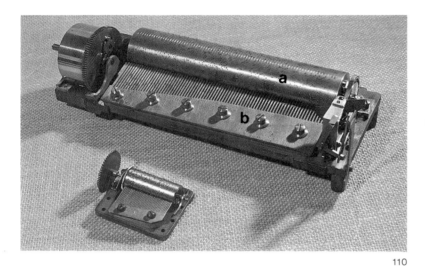

110

111

The Music of the Mechanical Doll

Nearly every mechanical doll possesed a musical component, operated directly by the main motor or sometimes by a small subsidiary one. The most frequent mechanism was the musical automaton, a cylinder and comb, invented in 1796 by the Genevan clockmaker Antoine Favre (110). The cylinder and comb has two principal elements, (a) a spiked drum

and (b) a musical comb, and can be miniaturized to fit into any subject (111). The drum has hundreds of spikes that lift up the teeth of the comb, and each tooth vibrates as it falls back, emitting a different sound. Also called orchetions, these devices come in every size; in complex pieces of musical furniture, they might set off gongs, bells, and other instruments. A melody is played by one complete revolution of the cylinder. To obtain a second tune, an ingenious device could move the drum

114

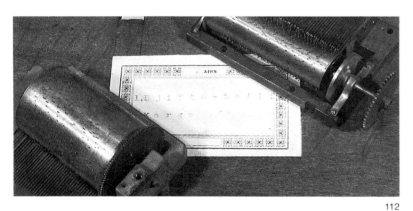

112

113

a dozen or so millimeters farther down the comb, thereby presenting a new series of spikes to the teeth. To produce a good tone in mechanical dolls, the musical device had to be placed in a sound box, which generally formed the base of the doll. A cylinder and comb placed in the body has poorer sonority, especially since the clothes and paper shells stifle the sound. Most of these musical devices played two melodies (112); mechanical dolls that played four, such

as the snake charmer (page 24) or harp-piano player (page 134), are rarer, and have very large drums (113). During the sixteenth and seventeenth centuries, organs were used in clock automatons (114), and were still in use for such large animated scenes as the orchestra of monkeys illustrated on page 124. In this orchestra, a large spilked drum opens and closes the valves supplying the organ pipes with air. The air is produced by a large wood and skin double-acting bellows

connected to a buffer-reservoir that regulates its output. A great deal of space was needed for this mechanism until about 1760, when Jaquet-Droz thought of replacing the organ pipes with a single tube, in which a moving piston produced a range of notes greater than an octave (115). The result was a flowering of extraordinary devices that, becoming smaller and smaller, were finally fitted into snuff boxes, watches, knobs of walking sticks, bottles, bracelets, and even

pistols. This mechanism is found in the whistling Gavrochinette. As this period, serinettes, little devices derived from this system, were made in great numbers; ladies used them to teach canaries to sing. Mechanical dolls representing birds that gave singing lessons were made by many, including Robert Houdin, famed primarily as a magician but also a talented clockmaker who invented mysterious clocks as well as mechanical dolls. The reputation of his marvelous works spread all

116

117

over the world and orders came from China (where they were called "singsongs"), from India of the maharajahs, and from the courts of Europe. In 1878, Edison invented the phonograph. A device inspired by the same principles was patented soon after by Lioret (116), who placed it in a number of talking dolls and mechanical doll musicians, such as the buglers, below. Every sort of gong, bell (117), flute, and dulcimer was to be found among the variuos musical devices in automatons. And

the greatest musicians, from Mozart and Handel to Stravinsky and Stockausen, unhesitatingly applied their talents to the music of the marvelous mechanical dolls of their times.

Harpist

After more than one hundred years of existence, this
musician by Vichy, 1855, still works with the original
pieces. His hands run over the harp strings, pluck them,
let go, and start again. His head and expression are
both mobile, and the harp is richly decorated. The
mechanism is installed in the body, along with a musical
cylinder and comb that play a simulation of the harp's
tune. This mechanical doll must therefore be classed as
a pseudomusician, since his gestures, although of
surprising dexterity, are only a pretense. Particularly
remarkable, his face is entirely covered with an
extremely fine leather. The eyelids, also of fine skin, are
equally animated. The doll is ninety centimeters high.

Guitarist

This guitarist is also an acrobat since he plays his instrument while balancing a peacock's feather on his nose. He turns the feather with virtuosity; it is inserted into a tube, which is visible in the photograph (123), along with a bell-crank lever and the pinions that turn it, at the top of the mechanism. The right arm that plays the guitar (122) and the head that balances the feather are also mobile. A little cord from the head works the eyelids (123). The mechanism is shown here in its original condition before restoration, for which the seams of the richly trimmed and embroidered costume were unstitched with infinite care. Time has left its mark upon the mechanism, which has about one hundred components (124). It is not surprising that the cylinder is so large (122), because music plays a major role in this automaton created by Decamps in 1895.

121

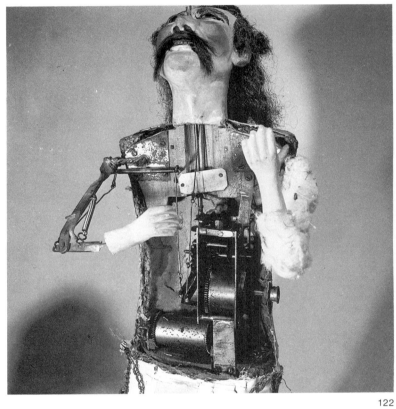

122

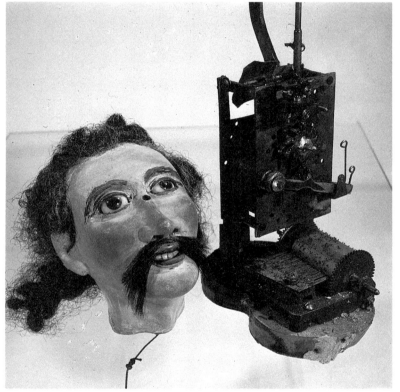

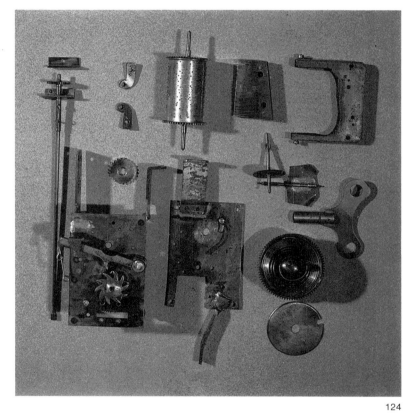

123

124

Large Orchestra of Monkeys

Nine musicians with their instruments are accomodated in this sizable piece of furniture, which stands 2.1 meters high. Two long-tailed monkeys plays the harp, three others play violin, and there is a cornet player, double-bass player, cellist, and percussionist in a blue uniform and cocked hat. The orchestra is gathered in a gallery of mirrors lit by a chandelier of crystal beads. The musicians follow their scores attentively, rolling their eyes as they play. The mechanism that animates each monkey's several gestures is made up of fifty cams, each producing a dozen different movements by means of the wires that pass through the floor into the monkey's bodies (126). An improved organ is lodged in the base of this automaton, which is hand driven by a crank. The giant skin bellows that provides compressed air for the organ pipes is set directly in motion by a crank arm. Air travels from the bellows into a sealed reservoir of wood and skin, which regulates its outlet before it moves into the sixteen wooden pipes. A cylinder seventy-one centimeters long, with thousands of points, works the forty-one valves that modulate the sound. By moving the roll laterally, it is possible to play eight different orchestral tunes. The levers are of iron, the pinions and cams of hardwood; the organ and cam shaft are linked by chains. It was created by Phalibois in 1880.

127

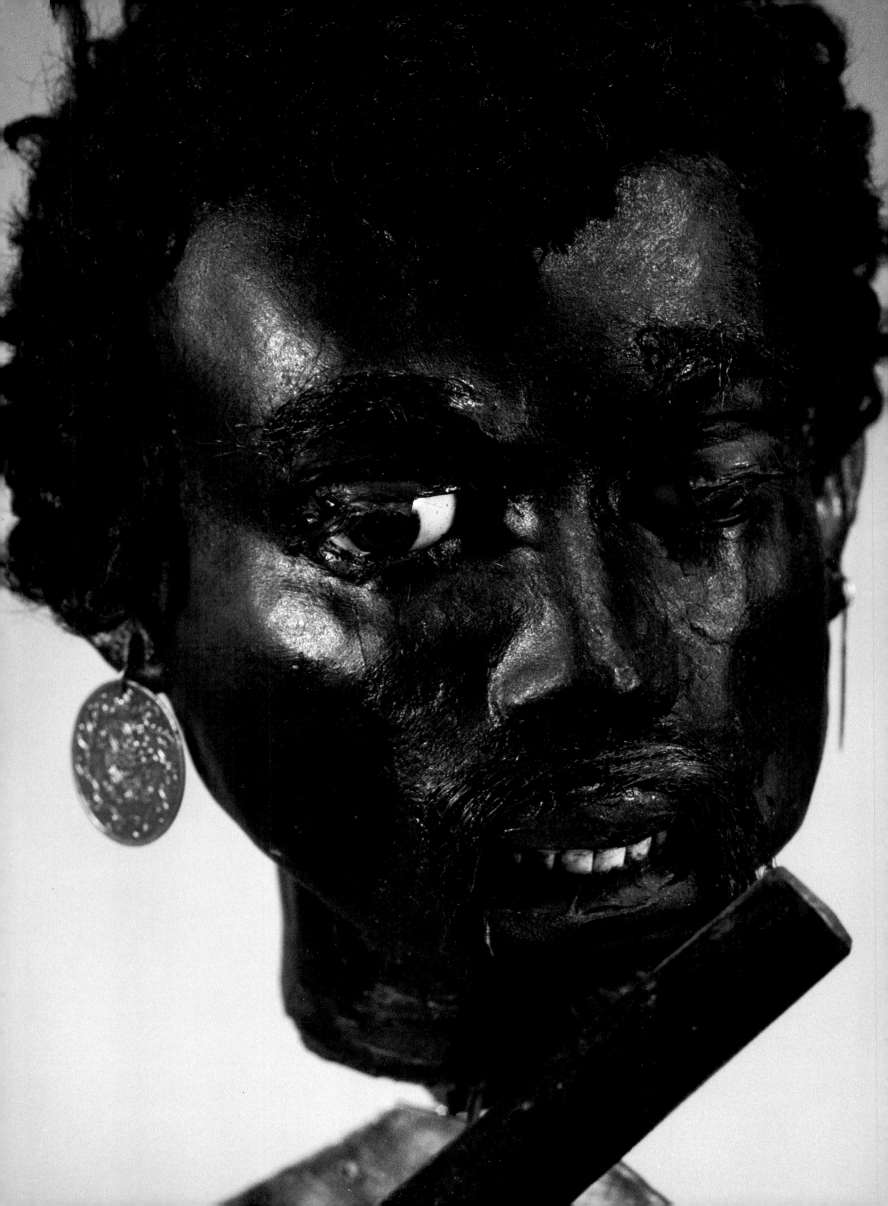

Flute Player

This mechanical doll belongs to a large family of Negro subjects much in fashion at the end of the nineteenth century. A whole series of black musicians was invented to satisfy the infatuated public. The mechanism of this one, made by Vichy in 1863, merits particular attention (129). Its spring-driven motor, derived from clocks, links directly to the plate that governs the figure's animation (130). Everything is enclosed in the papier-mâché body shell, which is covered with a black glaze. Seven cams turn at varying speeds. Through the diverse interactions of the steering gear, a large number of movements become possible: on the hands, for example, each finger is articulated (131, 132). The head is very expressive with its moving eyelids and mouth; the neck moves on two axes and can rotate and lean. The wheels are made of brass, but all other parts are of soft steel. This mechanical doll, eighty-three centimeters high, must be classed as a pseudomusician, since the flute does not actually play. A music box with a cylinder and comb provides the sound.

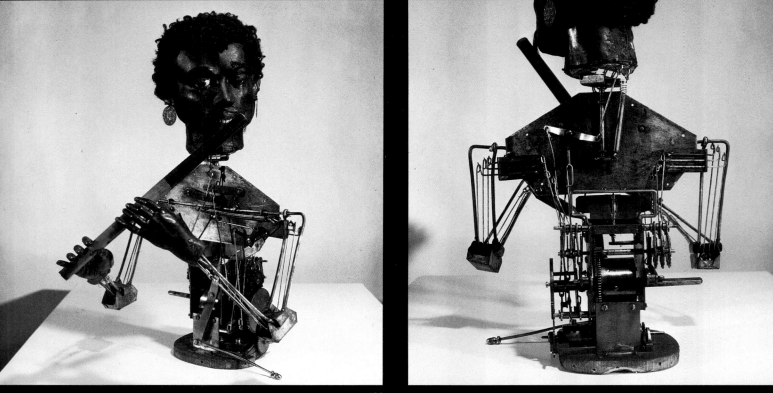

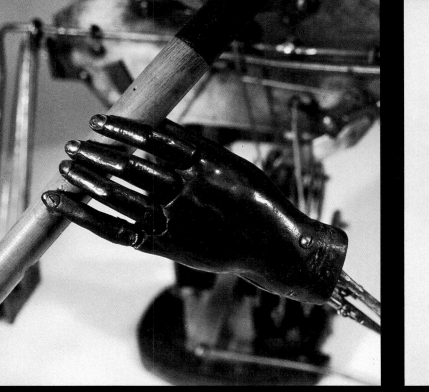

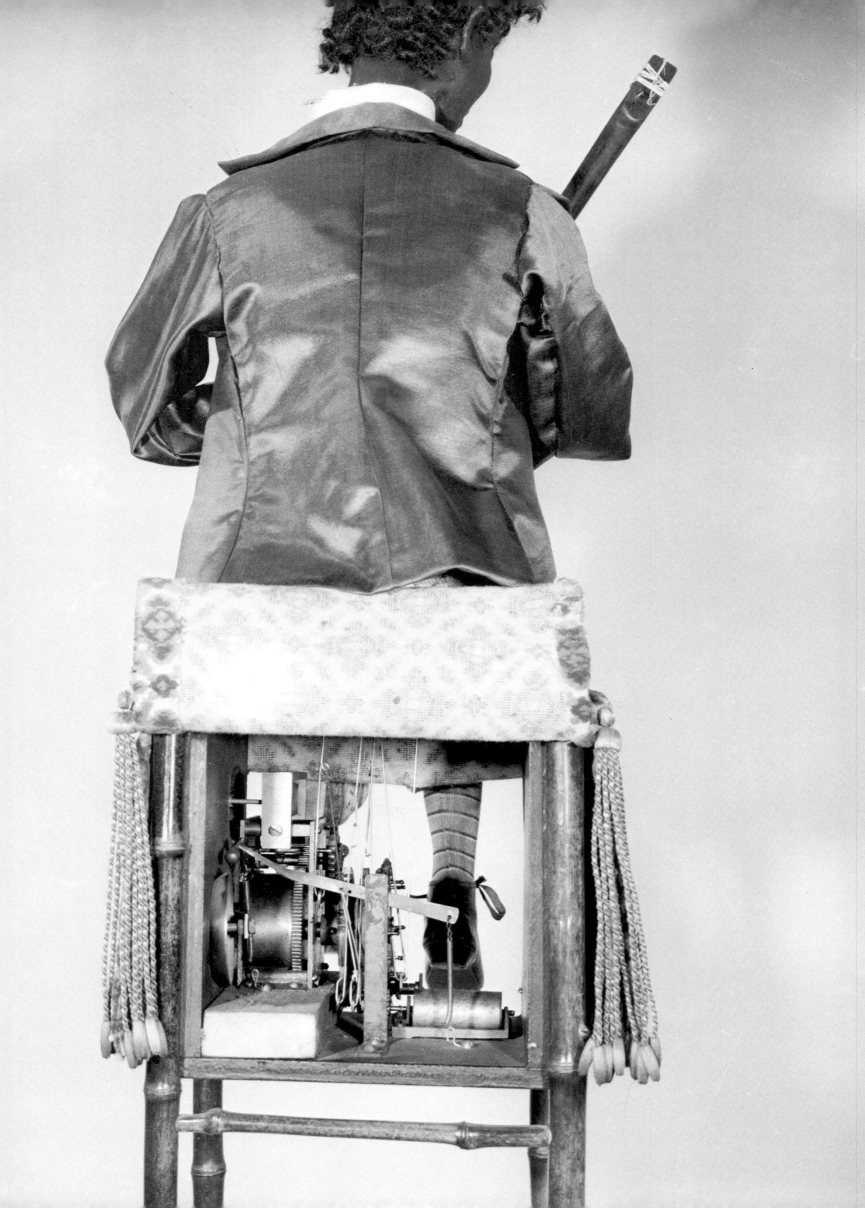

134

Banjo Player

This mechanical doll by Vichy, 1880, with its well-finished suit, leather shoes, and bonnet, belongs to the same family as the preceding one. Its instrument is also silent. The music comes from a cylinder and comb on the side of the mechanism, inside the seat of the stool, which serves as a sound box (133).

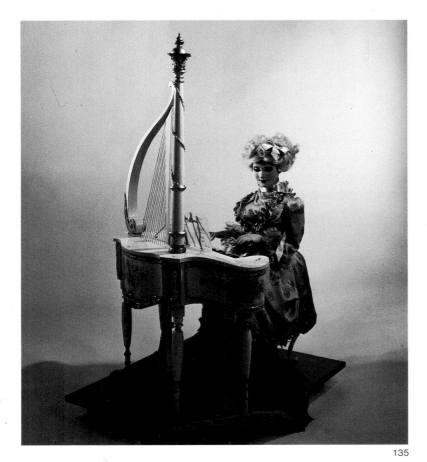

135

136

Harp-piano Player

This little marquise, who strokes the keyboard of the harp-piano with her fingers, belongs to the same category of pseudomusicians, but in this case the cylinder and comb are of exceptional size (136). The drum here is situated in the harp-piano itself, where a sound box amplifies sonority.

Altogether, the subject is quite large: the marquise measures eighty-six centimeters and the top of the harp-piano is a meter from the ground. The young woman's chest seems to breathe, and her head follows sometimes her fingers on the keyboard, sometimes the score of Schubert.

138

Monkey Violinist

Dressed in a gaudy coat, French breeches, a cocked
hat with pompons, and the monocle and powdered wig
of a marquis, this little monkey was made by Vichy in
1860. He plays his violin with a reckless air, as his eyes
roll at high speed in their sockets and his head turns to
every side.

Man with a Gong

Few mechanical dolls of this type have come down to
us. This tall figure (67 cm. high), created by Renoux in
Paris, 1890, moves along imitating a walk while hitting a
gong with the hammer in his right hand. His motion is
supplied by a three-wheeled trolley hidden under his
ceremonial dress, of a type worn in Africa during the
eighteenth century. A necklace of flowers conceals the
articulation of the neck. Eventually, such "walking"
mechanical dolls would be put on a table for greater
convenience and would fall to the ground and break,
thus ensuring their rarity today.

139

Spanish Guitarist

This guitarist by Lambert, with a pink biscuit-ware head and large black eyes, strums out a melody using diverse movements. She turns her head right and left, then tilts it forward. Her forearms are also mobile: her right hand brushes the strings and her left hand moves up and down the guitar neck. This mechanical doll has survived without changes; everything is original.

142

French Bugler

The musical mechanism of this bugler of Vichy's, made in 1880, is like that of the cylinder phonograph invented by Edison two years earlier, and prefigures today's record player. Through the action of wooden pulleys, the spring drives a cylinder covered with a layer of hard wax in which phonographic grooves are engraved. Above is a very light drum of thin cardboard with an open top to let the sound travel (116, page 117). On the drum is fitted a diaphragm with a point that reads the grooves. The drum moves as the point reads, and when the soldier takes his bugle from his mouth, the drum is lifted by an apparatus that returns it to the beginning of the grooves. The movement is repeated as long as the motor spring is wound.

143

Scottish Bugler

In a kilt of the colors of his clan, he blows the bugle while the flag goes up and down, worked by a halyard inside the pole. Vichy made this figure and its setting in 1880, using lacquered papier-mâché, and placed the simple mechanism in the bastion.

144

145

Drum Player

This figure, made by Decamps in 1880, is a real mechanical doll musician, eighty-three centimeters high. He beats an actual drum with his sticks, to a rhythm determined by the mechanism inside his body. His papier-mâché head is remarkably modeled and his eyelids are animated. Since arms, hands, and drumsticks must move rapidly and with some force in order to produce a rolling of the drum, the mechanism must overcome considerable inertia caused by the weight of these parts. Consequently, wear on the mechanism is the most crucial aspect of its conservation.

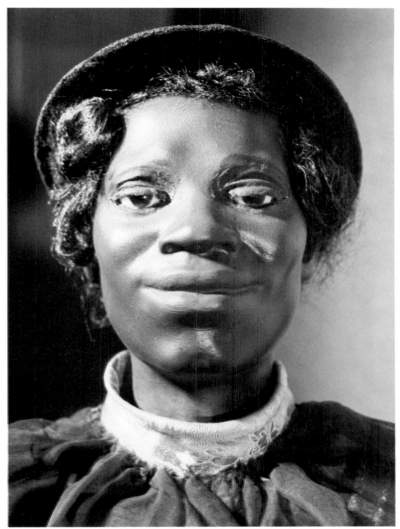

146

Pianist

This artist with biscuit-ware head and large blue eyes stands before the keyboard along which she moves her hands. Her head turns right and left in time to the music produced by a cylinder and comb. Heavy brown locks of real hair spread out over her wild-rose satin dress, set off with a black lace shawl. She was made by Lambert in 1865.

149

Choirboy

Dressed in a red cassock covered with a lace-bordered
white surplice and a short cape, this child takes a
collection for charity. With his left hand, he gestures
toward the alms box where a coin can be deposited
and thanks the donor with a nod of his head,
which has mobile eyelids. Not surprisingly,
this mechanical doll is coin operated.

145

151

Little Guitarist

The clothes of this mechanical doll are glued to the
papier-mâché body while the bolero an accessories are
sewn. The rosy-cheeked biscuit-ware head reminds us
that in most cases makers of mechanical dolls used
ordinary doll heads for their everyday creations. Only
the most exceptional figures had heads especially
sculptured ard molded. This little musician strokes the
strings of his guitar with porcelain hands, but the music
is produced by a cylinder and comb. The mechanism is
situated partly in his back, partly in the base.

Silhouettes of Soldiers

Of uncertain origin, these silhouettes of soldiers must have belonged to the shooting gallery of a nineteenth-century fair. Placed before a painted backdrop, they stand to attention with their bayonets when a marksman hits the target beneath them. Seventy-five centimeters high, they are made of cast iron; their mechanism is a simple hand-operated spring.

153

154

155

Conjuror with Fruit

Conjurors are frequent among the exotic figures. This one by Vichy, 1865, executes eleven different movements. An apple, pear, and peach are displayed on a plate. With a nod of his head, the conjurer draws the attention of the audience. The fruit topples over and a pair of lilliputian dancers appear inside the pear (154), an excited monkey winks from the apple, and a mouse trots from inside the peach. The mainspring mechanism is lodged inside the body of the mechanical doll itself, but a satellite mechanism situated beneath the tray animates the little subjects (155). While the whole piece is quite tall - sixty-five centimeters - the little dancers are only six centimeters. The head of the figure is mobile, and he seems to take the audience into his confidence as he goes about his tricks.

Couple with Parasol

A young lady seated on a red plush bench reads the page of a newspaper giving the results of the last elections. Blond with black eyes, she turns her head toward her neighbor, who opens out a parasol to protect her from the sun. At the couple's feet a long-eared spotted dog raises its head and wags its tail while looking at its masters. This mechanical doll by Phalibois works as soon as the crank is turned, providing both animation and a tune.

157

158

Lady with Mirror

This young lady with brown eyes stands before a mirror placed on a black wooden tripod. She powders herself with the powder puff in her right hand and leans forward to get a better view. Still powdering, she turns her head right and left, moves back, and straightens up. Her white satin robe decorated with lace hides a lace-bordered petticoat. She was made in 1890 by Decamps.

Landscape with Bird

The sails of windmill turn, a waterfall tumbles, a bird as big as the paddle wheel refreshes itself in the torrent, and in the foliage three other birds made of real feathers jump from branch to branch. In the grotto, two little figures, types of wise men, nod and wave their arms. A spring mechanism with a dozen cams and many pulleys and crank arms gives an intense life to every part of this landscape, from ground to treetop. The clock mechanism is independent of that which operates this scene devised by Bontemps in 1870.

Animated Picture

162

In a mountain landscape, a boat with large white sails stands out from the side of a lake. There are two little figures aboard: a young lady seated in the prow, and a standing sailor. The boat rocks to the movement of a blue paper wave. To the left, while the sails of a windmill turn, three simple animated figures dance in a mirror-walled grotto. Fixed to stems, they turn round and round on mobile legs. Designed by Phalibois in 1880, the landscape is animated to the tune of a musical cylinder and comb, which also drives the working parts. A wooden cam, fixed to the end of the cylinder, produces the pitching of the boat, while an eccentric gear, with a small iron wire crank arm, creates the choppy sea (163). A fishing wire that passes through a groove cut out in the wooden cam makes the dancers waltz and, rising up to the top of the picture, turns the sail of the windmill.

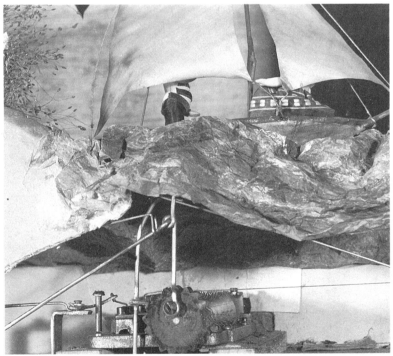

163

164

165

Landscape Beneath a Globe

This landscape by Phalibois, 1880, is embellished by a clock with an enormous dial. It comes to life with the sound of country music. The foreground couple turns and a paddle wheel to the left revolves in a direction opposite to the sails of a windmill overlooking the landscape. Further back, two little cutout cardboard silhouettes cross the scenery along a path (165). In the landscape background, painted directly into the globe, a church with a slate roof stands out from low red-roofed houses (166). A sense of depth is rendered by the winding pathway where two countrymen chatter.

166

Sentry with Bear

Decamps made this comic subject in 1900; the bear is about twenty-five centimeters high, the tree fifty-six. The bear is plush; the sentry and the rest of the scene is papier-mâché. The spring mechanism hidden in the base has a musical cylinder and comb. The sentry raises the roof of his sentry box with his head and sticks out his tongue several times while turning his head to one side. But the bear, well behaved, moves his mouth gently and leans amiably forward.

169

170

Dancing Couple

These two dancers in eighteenth-century costume were made by Vichy in 1875. They are mounted on a mechanism with three wheels enclosed in a metal shell. When the spring is wound and the piece placed on the ground, they turn round and round in close circles on the trolley hidden beneath her ample dress.

Dandy

This middle-size subject is by Phalibois, Paris, 1890. He stands eighty-seven centimeters high, with remarkable elegance and perfect bearing. Spick and span, he bends in the middle to bow, turns right and left to be admired, and, most comically, wriggles his tapered moustache. The mechanism in the base is particularly ingenious because the figure turns round and round. A little old-fashioned tune accompanies the movement.

172

173

Mechanism

The mechanism of a little eighteenth century clock. The mechanisms of mechanical dolls are, for the most part, derived from those of eighteenth and nineteenth century clocks.

Only meant to last as long as a toy, mechanical doll mechanisms were, with the exception of "chefs-d'oeuvre", more rudimentary than the mechanisms of clocks. Most frequently spring operated, they go back to the sixteenth century. The spring is enclosed in a drum (to the right of the photograph) which works the mechanism by means of a sprocket wheel.

174

Open drum with broken spring. The rupture of a spring often causes considerable damage because the resulting shock can break teeth off the pinions.

175

Spring operated mechanical doll mechanism, dismantled. An average mechanism has about a hundred pieces.

176

177

Air break mounted on a spring mechanism. The last pinion in the gearing system turns a fixed, fast turning screw to which is attached a "windmill" with two or four "sails" which breaks the unwinding motor spring.

The cam shaft is situated beneath (or worked by) the drive shaft. The cams are made of wood (box-wood), as in the above photograph, or of brass.

178

Brass cams. Each cam has a different profile, the number of lugs corresponding to its function. A cam animating the hands of a pianist will have a large number of lugs around its edge, while a cam working a body movement will be simpler.

179

The cams aligned along the cam shaft produce, by way of the wiring system, the various movements of the mobile organs of the mechanical doll.

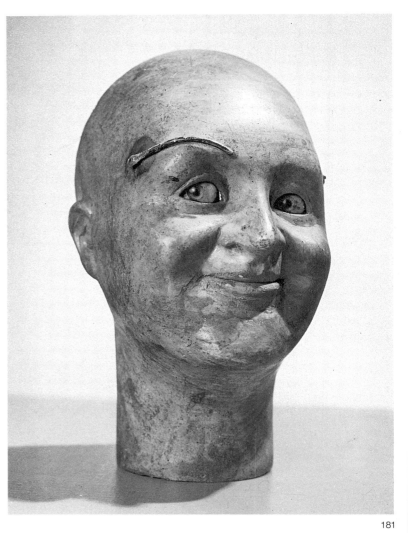

The Body of the Mechanical Doll

Whether it was to represent a shepherd or a prince, acrobat, monkey, or bear, each mechanical doll was first modeled as a sculpture of wood, clay, or wax. A mold of plaster or even cast iron was then taken. Fresh papier-mâché of boiled cardboard soaked in glue was then applied to this mold in as many layers as necessary to obtain a rigid shell. Holes were pierced in the shell so that the mechanism could be introduced. The entire back had to be cut out of larger figures. After the mechanism had been mounted, the half-shell was

readjusted with glue-soaked cardboard until the entire body had been solidly reconstituted. Thus, with all access to the interior blocked, restoration became impossible. In fact, repairs to the mechanism were not even foreseen, since each mechanical doll was meant to last only as long as it stayed in fashion. Wooden hands and feet were added to the cardboard body. The head, which was in most cases mobile, was extended from its supporting mandrel. The glossy appearance of the face was obtained by a lacquering of gutta-percha, ivorine, or both, and afterwards decorated.

The Restoration of Mechanical Dolls

When time comes to restore a mechanical doll, certain rules guide each step: preseve everything that can be preserved, conserve all original pieces, and as far as possible refrain from renewing the costumes of figures under the pretext that they are faded or soiled. Each of the antique dolls in the Galéa Collection represents part of the art and technology of a period. No one would think of repainting the Mona Lisa's gowns because the colors are a bit faded. As far as appearance, these automatons and animated dolls are in their own way as untouchable as the Mona Lisa. But mechanically they pose a thornier problem.

Certain restorations are necessary to bring life back to a mechanism that has stood up to the normal but ineluctable wear of time. In the last hundred years – the average age of the mechanical dolls in the National Museum at Monte Carlo – technology has evolved considerably. Materials are no longer the same, nor are the methods by which mechanical objects are assembled. Gearing systems have been standardized, as well as screw threads.

Mechanical dolls were for the most part unique works or were produced by artisans in a limited number of examples. Spare parts never existed, and neither standards nor rationalized production were known. It is not rare to find on the same bridge, or supporting piece, two screws of a different caliber! Nor were gears standardized: each wheel or pinion was cut with teeth of a different size. Further, the brass and steel formerly used have characteristics different from those found today. Before cutting a cylinder wheel, the workman of the last century had to beat a plaque of brass on an anvil, using the peen of a hammer to harden the metal and give it the desired mechanical resistance.

Today, when a part becomes irreparable, it must be remade in its former style, using the techniques of the period. Only the restorer who possesses an old tool, passed down from generation to generation, can hope to execute a gearing size faithful to that of the model.

The mechanism of mechanical dolls are derived from those used by clockmakers during the seventeenth and eighteenth centuries. But unlike clocks, which have a long, flexible spring to assure regular unwinding, often during a period of eight days, the mechanical dolls have the strongest possible spring in order to set in motion arms, legs, heads, and accessories infinitely heavier than the two hands of a clockface, and at speeds that are far from negligible. The spring of a mechanical doll moves about two hundred times faster than that of a clock! Consequently, the force exercised by the spring on the axes, bearings, wheels, and pinions is much greater, causing excessive wear cycle after cycle, until

All of these little trades have disappeared today, and the sources of raw materials have dried up. This irrevocable change makes these mechanical dolls, fragile tokens of bygone age, exceptionally interesting. The enormous difficulties faced by a restorer, who must be a mechanic, carpenter, model maker, painter, and dressmaker all at once, demand above all a passionate involvement on his part.

André Soriano

186

Index